LORD, GIVE ME A MAN!
Is That All You Want From God?

MAMIE WALTON
AND
LEVELLE T. WALTON

Copyright © 2015 by Mamie Walton

Lord give me a man!
Is that all you want from God?
by Mamie Walton

Printed in the United States of America

ISBN 9781629525013

All rights reserved solely by the author. The author guarantees all contents are original and do not infringe upon the legal rights of any other person or work. No part of this book may be reproduced in any form without the permission of the author. The views expressed in this book are not necessarily those of the publisher.

Unless otherwise indicated, Bible quotations are taken from Holy Bible, New International Version®, NIV® Copyright © 1973, 1978, 1984, 2011 by Biblica, Inc.® Used by permission. All rights reserved worldwide.

www.xulonpress.com

Table of Contents

Foreword ix

Dedication xiii

Introduction xv

Poem: For The Moment
by Monica Butts-Baker xviii

1. First Things First 21
   - Time With the Savior
   - No Condemnation
   - No Escape Clause
   - Terri's Testimony

2. D.A.T.I.N.G. 33
   - Christian Dating: Truth or Myth
   - Should We Be Doing This?
   - Breaking Up Is Hard To Do
   - Zamaya's Testimony
   - Get Yourself Together: Cooking

3. Bees Are Drawn To Honey. What Is
   Drawn To You? 49
   - Know Who You Are
   - My Testimony
   - Chandra's Testimony
   - Get Yourself Together: Cleanliness Is Next To Godliness: Part I

4. A Good Thing To Be Found. 67
   - Stop Looking Hungry
   - Lord, Please Don't Bend Over
   - Get Yourself Together: Cleanliness Is Next To Godliness: Part II
   - Jandalyn's Testimony: Marriage Preparation

5. Accountability 81
   - No Fancy Footwear
   - SLB's Testimony
   - Get Yourself Together: Cleanliness Is Next To Godliness, Part III

6. Single Parenting in Christ Is A Lie! 89
   - Pour It On
   - You Can't Be the Daddy
   - Let the Father, father
   - Watch Your Confession
   - Get the Little Buggers In Line

7. Redeeming the Time II: Self-Development 99
   - Get Out Of Town
   - Finances
   - Health

Table of Contents

- Kick It Up A Notch
- Get Yourself Together: Giving

8. Food For Thought...................... 109
   - No Hook Ups
   - Do Not Be Afraid To Fight
   - Time Lost
   - Redeem The Time (Ephesians 5:15)
   - Too Late To Turn Back Now
   - Cold Is Just Cold

9. From His Point Of View 121
   - I Know She Is Not The One
   - Levelle's Testimony

Summary............................. 131

Poem: You Can't Afford Me
by Monica L. Baker 133

Foreword

I enjoyed this book! Finally, here is a manual that addresses the very practical aspects of how to make yourself ready for making one of the most important decision of your life—-marriage.

As Mamie's pastor, I am grateful to see how the Lord has worked so powerfully in her to produce this wonderful book which stems from her own development and practice of life. I can tell you that she and her husband Levelle live out of the pages of this book. It is plain, to the point, and on a very non-religious, but certainly biblical foundation. Mamie pulls no punches! I love her wit and her humor. She tells it like it is.

This book is an important read for single people who are entertaining the thought of marriage. It is a major undertaking preparing oneself wholly for marriage but the results can be life changing. While preparing for marriage, I would suggest singles begin to gain an understanding that marriage is more than just companionship. It is a covenant between God, man and woman that should be taken seriously. Christian singles should also have a biblical perspective of marriage and the responsibilities that come with it. They should ask themselves, "What does God say about marriage? What does He say about divorce? Am I willing to commit myself to another according to scripture?"

Ephesians 5:25-33 commands, " Husbands, love your wives, just as Christ loved the church and gave himself up for her to make her holy, cleansing her by the washing with water through the word, and to present her to himself as a radiant church, without stain or wrinkle or any other blemish, but holy and blameless. In this same way, husbands ought to love their wives as their own bodies. He who loves his wife loves himself. After all, no one ever hated their own body, but they feed and care for their body, just as Christ does the church—for we are members of his body. For this reason a man will leave his father and mother and be united to his wife, and the two will become one flesh. This is a profound mystery—but I am talking about Christ and the church. However, each one of you also must love his wife as he loves himself, and the wife must respect her husband."

Marriage is about oneness and until your mentality changes from "I, Me, Mine" to "Us, We and Our," your relationship is off to a rough beginning. As a pastor, I have prepared many couples for marriage. We have discussed the principles of covenant and the importance of coming into the marriage with a healthy view of self and a clear sense of what to expect in building a lasting relationship. I must admit that there have been several times that I have wondered to myself if the couple I was counseling was well-suited for one another. I encourage couples who are serious about getting married, to engage in couple's counseling at least six months before the wedding and three months after. Counseling enables the pastor to address, with the couple, basic issues that deal with matters of companionship, oneness and challenges they are likely to face while building a solid foundation together. I also believe that if you follow the instructions of this book, you will know God's desire concerning your choice to marry and you will be prepared to live a joyful and wonderful life with the right person.

Pastor Raleigh Wingfield
Zion Assembly of Harrisburg, Pennsylvania

Dedication

Lord, thank you for taking time to come see about me one day. You are my life and the very air that I breathe. And with my every breath, I will praise you!

To my Mighty Man Of God, Levelle Truhart Walton. Thank you for believing in me. You are not only the man God has given me, but the man of God I asked for. We are God's divine best for one another, for better or worse, for richer or poorer, in sickness and in health, **until death do us part!**

To my son, Solomon Truhart Walton. May I set a godly example of a woman of God and as a wife to your father that would cause you to desire nothing less. May the blessings of God overtake you and may you walk in humility all the days of your life.

To my triplet brothers, Daniel and Alex Van Lee. Thanks for being the protective brothers that you are. I have learned much from you and will always love you. You are two of my greatest supporters in whatever I do.

To my aunt, Marguerite Brandt. Thanks for all you have taught me about etiquette and the importance of timing. You have always encouraged me to fulfill my purpose. You are an irreplaceable blessing.

To all the single women who have sat in my marriage prep classes. You have trusted me and I appreciate you. Don't settle for a counterfeit.

To Kimberly Hayes, Terri Sellers, Chandra Lewis, Shanie Johnson and Zamaya Johnson. You are my spiritual daughters, my princesses. I wish you were my own. I am unable to put into words how special you are to me. You occupy a special place in my heart. You are all women of God who are going places. Thanks for trusting the God in me as you seek my council. I love you.

To my Little Princesses Candice Wisdom, Indigo Sienna and Simone Arden Walton. Parenting you is my pleasure and you are my joy. All that I do is nothing if your lives are not impacted by the way I live my life before you. May I be a blessing to each of you while helping you grow into what God has for you. Mom loves you unconditionally.

And finally, to my chief editor April Wilson of **From Proof 2 Print**. Your fingerprint on this project was priceless. You know how to take a project from proof to print. Simply and sincerely, thank you.

Introduction

I started *A Good Thing to Be Found* several years ago to aid single women for the preparation and covenant of marriage. This is done in a five-part class consisting of one class a week in my home. Over the years, many single women have taken part in the class and have had life changing experiences.

While reading, you will come across testimonies from women who have taken these classes and benefitted from them. The purpose of the testimonies is to provide you an open window of the positive experiences these women have encountered due to their participation. Today, *A Good Thing to Be Found* has been called upon by many ministries to help them prepare their single members for marriage.

Throughout this book you will notice several scriptural references. Their purpose is to confirm what the Holy Spirit has given me to share with you. All scripture is quoted from the New International Version of the Bible.

It is my hope that this book, with the help of the Holy Spirit, will open your eyes to the areas in your life that need an upgrade as well as the areas in your life that need to be completely changed.

At the end of each chapter, you will find a section called, "Get Yourself Together!" These are areas of our lives that need to be addressed. Some may apply to you and some may not. Whichever the case, you are guaranteed to find <u>you</u> in there somewhere. When you do, please don't send me hate mail. Just be honest with yourself and Get Yourself Together!

Before going on, I would like to say that this book is not for everyone. It is for those who will admit that what they have been trying to do to get a husband hasn't worked. If you feel in your heart that you can keep doing the same things in hopes of getting a different result, you are mistaken. It is time to try something new. As you read through this book, please allow yourself to remain open and allow the Holy Spirit to have free reign to work in your heart. The goal is not to just read another book, but to change.

The scripture base for this study is Matthew 25:1-10. I encourage you to read this scripture as you embark on your journey of getting yourself together!

"At that time the kingdom of heaven will be like ten virgins who took their lamps and went out to meet the bridegroom. Five of them were foolish and five were wise. The foolish ones took their lamps but did not take any oil with them. The wise ones, however, took oil in jars along with their lamps. The bridegroom was a long time in coming, and they all became drowsy and fell asleep. At midnight the cry rang out: Here's the bridegroom! Come out to meet him! Then all the virgins woke up and trimmed their lamps. The foolish ones said to the wise, Give us some of your oil; our lamps are going out. No, they replied, 'there may not be enough for both us and you. Instead, go to those who sell oil and buy some for yourselves. But while they were on their way to buy the oil, the bridegroom arrived. The virgins who were ready went in with him to the wedding banquet. And the door was shut. Later the others also came. 'Lord, Lord,' they said, 'open the door for us!' But he replied, 'Truly I tell you, I don't know you.' Therefore keep watch, because you do not know the day or the hour."

Now that you have read the Scripture for your journey, let's get you prepared for marriage!

Lord give me a man!

For The Moment by Monica Butts-Baker

The awareness of aloneness causes anxiety in sobriety
So I seek to find togetherness in the drunkenness
Of infatuation. Even if
I sell my soul to the lowest bidder
Whose weightless words console the hollow ringing in my ears.
I fill up on calorie laden nutrition-less sound bytes
Because it fills me up,
When he feels me up,
For the moment, Baby.
For the moment, Baby.
When the moment turns into wasted time,
I am aware of my foolishness.
So I rationalize my self- mutilation,
My deterioration,
My breakdown.
Now let me break it down.
The awareness of my separateness,
Leads to unions of conformity;
Yields deformity
When the reality
Of the matter, see,
Is that I just want to be
LOVED!
But at what price do I sacrifice
For the void in my life?

So I turn to the Creator, but not right now; I'll do that later
After I'm done with the things he wants to do to me,
Get all that out of me,
So when I'm done I'll be
So fresh and so clean clean.
No!
So empty...back to reality....some kind of clarity
Brokenness leads to wholeness-Totality
Keep finding myself left with my self.
Better get some help and learn to love myself;
Don't expect no one else to love me 'till I love myself.

- 1 -
First Things First

I want you to set this book down and take a good look at yourself in a mirror – not at the pimples or perhaps even that nose that you feel is too big or that chipped tooth, but you the person. With all the flaws you think you have, there are men out there that will accept you. Men are not all that choosy. You can get a man if that is all you want. However, if you are tired of being another man's girlfriend, engaging in dead end relationships filled with compromise and later condemnation, I suggest you prepare yourself to be challenged by what this book has to say. There are so many things we want and desire in life. Some of us dream about them while others pursue and obtain. Before we seek or pursue one more thing, we must first pursue and obtain salvation.

For those who have not considered making the Lord Jesus Christ their Lord, the word of God says to

"Seek first the kingdom of God and His righteousness and all these things will be added to you" (Matthew 6:33). God wants us to desire Him more than things. We must realize that things are temporal, but where we spend eternity is forever. When we don't have salvation, Christ on the inside, we use things to fill the place in us that is crying out for a Savior. Nothing purchased or given can satisfy you like Christ can. No man will either. God says: "Behold, I stand at the door and knock. If anyone hears my voice and opens the door, I will come in to him and dine with him, and he with Me" (Revelation 3:20).

Make Christ your Lord and Savior today by asking Him to come into your heart and cleanse you from all sin. Ask Him to show you how to live for Him. God will give you the things you desire, but you need Him first. If you already know Christ, great! You will get to know the Savior and grow in Him when you spend time in His word and in prayer. Don't forget that a relationship with God must come before any other relationship.

Time with the Savior

Spending time with God is an essential key to growing into the woman God has called you to be. It is also a key element in the life of a believer who desires to be married. I can assure you that men of God are not praying for a wife who has no prayer life. A real man of God desires a woman that has some experience touching heaven. It is vital to the marriage relationship of a believer. You must understand that it is not what is visible to the human eye that causes women to be considered a "good thing", but rather what is on the inside. The inside is always reflective of the time we spend or don't spend with God. It happens to show up in the things that we say and do.

How much of a priority is God in your life? There is a song called *I Miss My Time with You* that speaks on how believers used to spend time with God, but now are too busy serving out of an empty vessel. In order to be placed in the category of a "good thing", we must realize that a true man of God desires a woman who already has an established relationship with God that involves a lifestyle of spending time in the face of God.

What kind of relationship do you and God have if you are not in conversation with Him? You need not seek or believe God for a powerful anointed man of God if your life doesn't line up with God's word. You have no right to expect a powerful man of God to come into your life and ask for your hand in marriage if you are living outside of God's will for your life.

Woman of God, it is time for you to kneel down. God has much to show you and so much to say to you; but first, you must be in the position to hear His voice. When you take the time to acknowledge God, you will be surprised at what He has to say to you. Let's take our focus off men for a while and ask God to do a new thing in us.

While you are single, you have advantages most wives only hold dear as a memory. One such advantage is having the opportunity to pray anytime you want. When you are single, you can seek God at all hours of the day or night without interruption. If you are married, that opportunity is not always available. If you are married, your husband may prefer to feel the warmth of your well-manicured toes instead of the folding of praying hands. Times may come when praying is not on your husband's mind. If that is the case, you may have to wait to pray.

"I would like you to be free from concern. An unmarried man is concerned about the Lord's affairs—how he can please the Lord. But a married man is concerned about the affairs of this world—how he can please his wife— and his interests are divided. An unmarried woman or virgin is concerned about the Lord's affairs. Her aim is to be devoted to the Lord in both body and spirit. But a married woman is concerned about the affairs of this world—how she can please her husband. I am saying this for your own good, not to restrict you, but rather you may live in a right way in undivided devotion to the Lord." - (I Corinthians 7:32-35)

Another advantage to being single is being able to go on a spiritual fast anytime you choose. You can fast whenever you want for as long as you want and I would encourage you to do just that. Fasting can be one of your greatest weapons. Just keep in mind that if you are married and decide to go on a fast, you are to consult with your spouse first. In the event your spouse agrees with your fasting, be careful not to be on a lengthy fast so as not to give the enemy an open door into your marriage.

You may not agree with the part about consulting with your spouse before fasting, but if you desire to be a woman after God's own heart, and want to line up with the word of God, you will obey what the word states in I Corinthians 7: 5: Do not deprive each other except perhaps by mutual consent and for a time, so that you may devote yourselves to prayer. Then come together again so that Satan will not tempt you because of your lack of self-control.

You must come to terms with the fact that marriage is a lot of things, including a sacrifice. If you are going to get hung up on the fact that you will have to clear it with your husband before going on a fast, then enjoy being single. If being subject to your husband in this manner is of genuine concern to you, allow me to suggest a book that will set you free: *Liberated Through Submission* by P.B.Wilson (Harvest House Publishers, 2006). This book taught me that there is freedom in submission, not bondage.

No Condemnation

One of the chief reasons for writing this book is to help prevent divorce. Please, don't put this book down because I used the "D" word. Allow me to talk about it for a moment. I promise to be quick.

If you have been through a divorce then you can confirm that it was not one of your most memorable moments. Your marriage has ended and you hate the fact that things did not go the way you had planned. Well, guess what? God says he hates divorce, too. This point is proven in Malachi 2:16, which states, "I hate divorce", says the Lord, God of Israel, "Because the man who divorces his wife covers his garment with violence."

Many women who have been divorced often find it hard to both trust and to fully give of their hearts because of the damage incurred by divorce.

Believers have often felt that they have a "biblical right" to divorce. This assumption stems from the scripture found in Matt. 5:31-32 which states: "It has been said, 'Anyone who divorces his wife must give her a certificate of divorce.' But I tell you that anyone who divorces his wife, except for sexual immorality, makes her the victim of adultery, and anyone who marries a divorced woman commits adultery."

Allow me to present the fact that there is no such thing as a "biblical right." God permits divorce in the case of unfaithfulness if our hearts are hardened. That "exception to the rule" falls under the permissive will of God and not His perfect will.

The permissive will of God always involves God getting less glory or no glory at all. The permissive will of God doesn't mean that God is pleased with your decision. He simply will allow it because there is no place in your heart to allow Him to do what He truly desires. God desires you to work through the areas of your heart that need healing. There are times when God will allow us to do what we want, even if it does not bring Him glory.

While it may be hard to do what is right by honoring the vows you made in the company of witnesses and in the presence of Almighty God, you must remember that you are an example to single women of what a godly wife should be.

Before I was married, I overheard a group of single people having a conversation about how they believed Christian marriages were not expected to last long because of the increasing divorce rate. They also believed many Christian marriages failed because there were not many successful marriages to prove otherwise. We who are married have an obligation to do all that we can to make sure our marriages last. The "happily ever after" aspect of a marriage is one that you create and build.

The world makes obtaining an uncontested divorce as simple and as affordable as $250. I have seen it advertised on many billboards and I am sure you have too. Have you ever noticed how miserable and sad the divorcing couple looks on those billboards? What is even sadder is that many believers often seek the council of an attorney to end their marriage rather than the council of God to save it. When a husband and wife have agreed to divorce, an attorney can not make their covenant go away. Believers, we can do better than that.

If you have been divorced, regardless of who was at fault, the word of God tells us that there is no condemnation to them who are in Christ Jesus (Romans 8:1). This book is not designed to take you back into your old way of thinking, but to help you move forward with a new mindset in Christ. It may call for you to reflect upon or face old behaviors. Do not be fearful of this process. Reflection is not to keep you in the past; it is intended to propel you forward towards a more positive change. Reflection will also allow God to change those old destructive behaviors that have kept you bound in sin.

Before going further, allow me to add a little disclaimer. I am Mamie Walton and the word of God is the Word of God. I have taken time to provide you with a few scriptures on the issues of divorce for you to meditate upon. What I think about divorce will never be as important as what God has to say about it. Ask Him first. Allow God to be the one you consult. When I discuss an issue with a mentor or a close friend, it is not for the purpose of getting direction for my life, but for the purpose of confirmation.

When I was a little girl, I didn't know if God was real. My conversation with God began like this, "God, if you are real…" Once I found out that God was real and that He had power to do things on the earth and in my life, I changed my conversations. I consulted Him about everything. I am still that way today. I consult Him on topics ranging from raising my children to how I should do my hair.

Therefore, when it comes to something as serious as divorce or how to care for our marriages, we should consult the heart of God. You can hear the heart of God through conversations with another believer. I advise you to make sure that it is God's heart you are hearing and not the heart or opinion of the person to whom you are speaking. If that person should happen to lead you in the wrong direction, blaming them won't change the potential disaster of your situation. Always seek God first.

Many times, women will consult with me about an issue pertaining to their single status. Before addressing the issue, I always ask them this very important question: "Do you want to hear the heart of God or my heart?" I do not want my retelling of personal experiences to mingle with what God has need for them to hear. If I pray to ask God to give me the words that will honor Him, then the chances are greater that I will say the right things. Please pray before you read the following scriptures and always remember that it is important to know what the word of the Lord says:

Genesis 2:8, 18 "Now the Lord God had planted a garden in the east, in Eden; and there he put the man he had formed. The Lord God said, 'It is not good for the man to be alone. I will make a helper suitable for him.' "

Malachi 2:16 "The man who hates and divorces his wife," says the Lord, the God of Israel, "does violence to the one he should protect," says the Lord Almighty. So be on your guard, and do not be unfaithful."

Mark 10:9 "Therefore what God has joined together, let no one separate."

I know that this is a hard saying but God hates divorce!

No Escape Clauses

Marriage is a covenant, a vow between three persons: a man, a woman and God. This covenant says that all the things that constitute our wedding vows we will keep by the power of God. We are vowing to stay in the marriage for better or for worse, for richer or for poorer, in sickness and in health, until death do us part.

With these vows in mind, let us properly prepare ourselves before entering into a covenant as sacred as marriage.

The life of a believer is constantly on display. The world truly expects us to be different from them. Many who are of the world spend more time and money planning for a wedding ceremony that lasts for just a day than they do on the marriage that is supposed to last a lifetime. Those who do not understand the three-cord ribbon philosophy of the Bible will consider the breakup of their marriage as another part of life and keep it moving. Believers must not take this attitude. We must see that God holds us to a higher level of accountability.

Accountability. It means, "I have spoken my vows and made a covenant before God and witnesses. I will, with God's help, do all that I can to make sure my marriage lasts."

A wise man once described the covenant of marriage this way. "You have things God has called you to do and I have things God has called me to do and we agree to do them together. The rest is up to Him."

I often tell my husband that I want to one day, when my hair has gone totally gray, look over at him in bed and see that his hair has gone gray, too. What I am saying is that he is the only man that I desire and want to grow old, happy, and content with.

If you want the same thing with your man of God, then I suggest you develop a new mindset that does not entertain the idea of divorce but one of covenant.

Levelle and I have agreed to never use the "D" word in our marriage. If we are to remain as a couple, we must have safeguards in place so as not to violate our agreement. We do what works for us. I hope you will do what works for you when the time comes.

I believe that most couples respect being in a covenant, while others have no concept of honoring anything. Start now by changing the way you look at it. If you tell someone you will call them tonight, call them. If you say you will be there, be there! If you sign up for a committee, see it through from start to finish. If you sign up for a team sport, complete the season and don't quit halfway through it. The team depends upon you and should be able to count on you. When we sign on the dotted line, we fail to realize it is the same as our word.

Practice keeping your word by starting today. Try to be more aware of how many times you break your word on a daily basis. If you find that you break your word more often than you keep it, repent to both God and that person, and then seek a more honorable way to live.

Terri's Testimony

Levelle and Mamie Walton are the epitome of true godly love. I know because they adopted me as their spiritual daughter seven years ago and I have seen it firsthand. The information they teach is from experience, and every class is different. The truth they present is clothed in love and wisdom from the Lord. Mamie Walton is a relationship expert on what a woman or a man can do to prepare for marriage. She speaks from the heart of God.

My testimonial of the "Get Yourself Together" class is that it is life changing, very practical, and will prepare any woman to be "God's divine's best." In this life, where there are so many avenues to meet a companion, there is a little black book that details the dos and don'ts on preparing for a healthy marriage. We have done it wrong as a society. We've allowed ourselves to become emotionally involved without commitment. My loving parents address all these issues in their book, Lord, I Want A Man! They practice what they preach and this book will mature you and enhance your life. I am stronger and wiser because of their teachings. The women that I interact with about my views on dating and trusting God are astounded by my words and they listen because they know it is the God in me.

The greatest thing I have learned is that no matter your background, ethnicity, or past, my spiritual mother's book will prepare any woman to be a dedicated wife who will be dearly loved by her husband. My life and the lives of dozens of other women are more fulfilled as a result of her leadership and the material she teaches.

Love you ma and poppa Walton. Thank you for your wisdom.

Warm Regards, Terri

-2-
D.A.T.I.N.G.

Deadly Attempt To Imitate the Nature of God and God's Love

Webster's Dictionary defines *boyfriend* as a frequent or regular male companion in a romantic or sexual relationship. It also defines *romance* as, "Conducive to or suitable for lovemaking" and sexual as, "Having or involving sex."

This chapter is devoted to the whole issue of dating. By now, you are probably ready to skip this chapter and go on to the next one, unless you find out that what I am going to say makes sense and may require you to change. Come on, we are mature women of God, right? All I ask is that you hear me out.

Christian Dating: Truth or Myth?

Christian dating is no more than following after the lustful desires in our hearts that strokes the desires of our flesh. Following after these desires allows us to explore how close we can get to the fire without being burnt. Christian dating has no track record of being a tool for a stronger relationship in Christ, but rather a damaging one. In so doing, it presents itself as another stronghold that must be torn down in the life of the believer. When we cry out for the right to date, it is no more than our flesh crying out because it can't have its own way. The only way we can silence our flesh is to deprive it of what it needs to live. Stop taking orders from your flesh!

Ladies, when the women of God take on the actions or behaviors of the world, they should expect nothing more than the same results as the world gets. It is not God's plan for us to adopt the ways of the world; in spite of God's command to not be conformed to this world (Romans12:2), we continue to do so, then question God when we begin to reap the harvest based upon what has been sowed. If you have left the world don't return to it.

During the transition of moving out of worldly living and into kingdom living, it should be noted that certain behaviors must cease. Although the new believer has chosen a new way of life, those behaviors that were once accepted in the world now become a snare. The good news is with the help of the Holy Spirit, new believers will begin to become acutely aware of what behaviors are acceptable to God, and what are not.

As they grow in their relationships with God, the Holy Spirit will begin to reveal what is of God and what is of the world. As our guide and pattern for living, the Bible gives examples of couples coming together. Yet there are no examples of fathers giving their daughters to men as girlfriends. There were no romantic candlelight dinners and abstinence classes.

As we get to know the Lord more, there will be behaviors and issues that will begin to shed. The Holy Spirit will begin to free us up and allow us to be used by God on a greater level. For example: If you are a thief when you get saved, then you may sense the Holy Spirit convicting you every time you steal. He is trying to bring you to a place where you no longer desire to engage in such destructive behavior.

Now, let's say you like to frequent bars to party and have a drink from time to time. God will begin to direct you in another way or He may just take the desire to frequent bars away from you. There are times when you know that you are doing something that does not honor the Lord; but to tear yourself away from it will be painfully hard. You realize that the only way you are going to remain obedient to God is to release that habit or behavior to Him and ask Him for grace. It's not easy but you can do it.

Then there are times that the handwriting is on the wall. All the signs are there and you know that what you are doing is not what God intended for your life. Because you enjoy what you are doing, you continue to compromise. You constantly get burned over and over, and yet, you still won't turn it over to God until you get a revelation that God is not honored in your actions. You then begin to realize in order to go to the next level you must change. Dating does not honor God. To go to the next level, you will need to adopt a new mindset when it comes to with whom you share your heart and body.

Past dating experiences have taught you that dating can bring heartache. Why would you want to bring the concept of dating with you into the body of Christ? Doing so leaves room for sin. You may not agree with what I am saying because you are dating Christian men and you don't plan to do in your "Christian relationships" what you have done in your "worldly" relationships. Save it! This is not a Christian relationship. The whole idea of dating comes from the world. Given enough time, the right circumstances, and the right location, you <u>will</u> do the same things in Christ that you did in the world.

You should understand that biblically, there is no such thing as "Christian Dating." Think about it for a moment. If the definition of a boyfriend is a *frequent or regular male companion in a romantic or sexual relationship and romance is conducive to or suitable for lovemaking*, how can Christians engage in dating? Dating satisfies the flesh and we were instructed to crucify the flesh, not romance it. To do otherwise is dangerous. When you get a revelation that "Christian Dating" is a deception, you will begin to walk upright as a single woman of God. No compromise, just holy. That is how your time should be spent anyway, living holy with no room for compromise.

There is so much compromise in dating for believers. Sinners sin so we shouldn't consider that to be a big deal. There must be no compromise in the life of a believer. Dating is just that, dating, and is not biblical. One may say that this idea is too old-fashioned. Things are different now. I say the word of God never changes. The time you spend opening yourself up to compromise, sharing yourself with men in the body of Christ as you did with men in the world, could be better spent in the presence of God. This time should be spent being remade as a woman of God in preparation for marriage.

Growing up in Christian households, our parents spent time encouraging or even demanding that we not engage in sexual intercourse. Why? Because they did not want us to get pregnant and bring them shame. On the other hand, very little was taught about the body being the temple of the Holy Ghost (the place where He abides), or about not defiling it so not to dishonor the Lord. There is not much said these days about keeping one's self for marriage.

If you were to ask parents if they taught their daughters to keep themselves for marriage by abstaining from sex, I bet most would say that they have. If the truth was told, the right answer would be NO!

The monologue between most parents and their daughters is often brief. The primary focus of the conversation is to encourage them not to bring home a baby, and not to shame the family, or lessen the daughter's chances of going to college. What about sexual purity? We can't adopt the worldly idea of dating and expect our daughters to remain sexually pure. Can we be that naive? Sexual purity means to be untouched and unhandled, belonging to the Lord only until marriage. Just as the Ark of the Covenant housed the glory of God, so our bodies house the spirit of the living God. Shouldn't we then take heed to how we handle or who we allow to handle our bodies? We live in a day and age where we handle China with more care than our temples. We go on to teach our children to do the same.

When dating, we usually find ourselves engaging in some form of sexual compromise, such as kissing, petting, manual stimulation and/or oral sex. We don't talk about it, but girl, you know I'm right. Sadly enough, these acts are not considered compromises. It is what we do when we date and all of it, at some point in the relationship, can be expected. In many cases, we don't even see the wrong in it until the act is over and the condemnation begins. If you go long enough ignoring the voice of God on the inside saying, "Girl, you know you shouldn't be doing this," your level of compromise will be greater the next time, and before you know it, you've given in.

When we compromise who we are and our beliefs, our lives are no longer set a part from the lives of those who are of the world. Just as they sit in church trying to attempt some form of godliness when all the while choosing to do their own thing, believers who choose to compromise their walk with God in order to fulfill the lust of the flesh also sit in church with a form of godliness but lacking the power thereof. The compromising believer can no longer worship with a pure heart because of her compromising ways. She tries to look like everyone else around her but her heart is hardening toward the things of God. If you are that compromising believer, you are well aware that your walk is not like it used to be. You continue to deceive yourself into thinking that God would not want you to break the guy's heart with whom you have a committed relationship. I'd like to relate a story to you of a woman who compromised her beliefs in order to have a relationship with a man.

A woman I am acquainted with told me of the time she entered into a relationship with a man who was mourning the death of his mother. She entered into the relationship because she felt sorry for him that he had no one left. After they began seeing each other, the man began to pressure her for sex. He told her that since they both wanted each other in that way and were committed to one another and planned to be married (he handed her an engagement ring), they were doing nothing wrong. He assured her that God would understand.

Flattered and excited at the sudden marriage proposal as well as afraid that she would lose him if she continued to fight the desires developing in her own heart, she gave in. After that first night, having sex became a part of their relationship. His next move was in suggesting that she move in with him. He reasoned that since she was at his house most of the time, she should move in so that they could see more of each other. Thinking that the relationship was going somewhere, she gave up her small apartment and moved in to his.

During this time, the woman was only going to church on the Sundays she was off from work. After a while, she stopped asking for Sundays off. It gave her an excuse to miss church and she felt justified. After living this way for only a short while, the man grew tired of feeling like he had to check in and account for his actions like he were married when in fact, he was a single man. Abruptly, things ended when he told her that he wanted to explore other relationships, and would prefer they part as friends.

Since she had given up her apartment to live with him, she had no place to go and ended up moving back home with her mom. It wasn't long after the breakup that she learned that she was expecting. The man wanted nothing to do with a baby and encouraged abortion. November of that year she gave birth to a son who will be raised without a dad. I asked her if the compromise was worth the consequences. Her reply? No.

Almost every single Christian woman reading this book can relate to this story in one way or another. You can agree that there were times when you felt uncomfortable engaging in acts that eventually led to sexual impurity. Allow me to offer a solution to the problem: STOP DATING. Why reduce yourself to the title of "girlfriend?" Why open yourself up to a world of potential mess in an attempt to fill a void that only God can fill?

Ladies, men will sleep in your bed, wash off in *your* shower and Use *your* personal bar of soap. While in there, he will acknowledge that being with you is not good enough to fill the void. They will get a revelation, while in *your* shower, that God is doing a new thing. In an attempt to step it up, they will cry out to God for a change, for a wife. They will dry off their behind with *your* towel, drop it on *your* floor and roll out. Looking for a wife and not a quick temporary fix, they will filter every encounter through different eyes, the kind that can spot a wife. You will not be one of the contenders because you, my friend, were one of his flavors of the month. You have been filed away in his rolodex. When a serious man of God seeks a wife, he never thumbs through the rolodex.

The time between your desire for marriage and your wedding day should be given to preparation for God's divine best for you and not in the giving of your heart. You deceive yourself by saying, "Well, the most we do is hold hands and maybe kiss." You have no business swapping DNA with anyone other than your God-appointed husband. Save what you have left for marriage!

Breaking Up Is Hard To Do

Dating is an almost guaranteed heart break. You will unfortunately continue to go into relationships thinking that each one is *the* one. Think about it. Almost every guy you dated and broke up with has affected your heart in at least some small way. You cried, were angry and hurt. Meanwhile, he has showered and moved on. We are emotional creatures and we usually find it hard not to give a man our heart. It just happens. On the flip side, there are those women who find it hard to give a man their heart. These are the women who rarely get hurt by break-ups. Unfortunately, what they fail to realize is that their ability and willpower in not allowing their heart strings to form comes from the fact that they have already been hurt. They have and will always have these carefully constructed walls they carry around, unpacking and installing, in every relationship they engage in. And when the relationship is over, they take down the walls and pack them away for the next relationship. If you are that type of woman, you are really messed up and don't even know it. While this type of woman appears to be taking the safe route, she will have problems in marriage if she doesn't learn how to let people in. She must learn what a healthy relationship is. It involves allowing herself to love. (I am not referring to a romantic relationship).

Break-ups hurt because they generally involve giving a part of our hearts to every man we date, which allows each man to walk away with a piece of our heart. When we finally encounter the man of our dreams, the one to whom we vow to share our whole heart with, we utterly come to the realization that pieces of our hearts are scattered among several men. This is not God's plan for your life. God wants us to give our hearts fully to our husbands. When we give away pieces of our hearts to other men, we often come to the marriage with ideas reflective of our past relationships and heartbreaks.

Now that you are married to Mr. Right, what do you do when something happens in your marriage that conflicts with what your beliefs of what a marriage should be? You are ready to call it quits and file for a divorce. Why? Because when you were dating, what you were actually doing was preparing yourself for divorce! In your singleness, when things didn't work out, it was over. If a better flavor came along then your current relationship was over. Now that you are married, and things aren't going the way you would like, you consider divorce. You say to yourself there are more fish in the sea. What you really want is the one who caught you. You just don't have the right tool on your belt to maintain the marriage. The world expects more from us than that. I was told by a believer once that if a woman thinks a guy is going to break up with her, she does the breaking up first. This way, she can have the satisfaction of dumping him instead of being the one to get dumped. Sounds crazy, but it is just an example of a mind not totally yielding to God. If you don't get entangled with the ways of the world (dating), being dumped won't be an issue for you.

If we continue to date, we are showing the world that there is no difference between them and us. We are commissioned to show them the difference. Unfortunately, we are too busy doing all we can to be like the world and we don't even realize it. If there is no difference in our lives and in our witness, how are we to win the world for Christ? It is certainly not through our examples.

Again, I am not condemning anyone who has been through a divorce. It happens. If you are to ever have a successful marriage, there are some things that need to be addressed and changed in order to make better decisions in the future. First, it is important to separate the word dating from the word courting. Dating involves being open to the fact that you are opening yourself up for the potential to fall into sin. As we discussed earlier, dating leads to romance. It clearly opens the door for intimacy and belongs in marriage. Courting, on the other hand, says the two of you are declaring you plan to be joined together as husband and wife. The purpose of your time together is to become more familiar with one another before getting married. It should be noted, although the courtship will eventually lead to marriage, the couple should avoid being alone to avoid tempting situations that could lead to sinning.

Second, the desires of our flesh are what makes it hard to grasp the idea of a man of God coming to a godly woman and making his intentions, or desire to marry her, known. The flesh is so used to being toyed with that we feel we must give in to its desire to have a romantic relationship with a man instead of holding on to our standards as godly single women. To keep from falling into sin, we must crucify our flesh. We cannot afford to fulfill the lusts of the flesh; we must crucify it. In Galatians 5:24-25, the Apostle Paul teaches that those who belong to Christ have crucified the affections and lusts of the flesh. If we live in the Spirit we must also walk in the Spirit. Crucifying the flesh will free you, the believer, from sin. In the process, it will allow God to work on you for the purpose of marriage. There is so much He can show you and do in you during this time; be willing to get to work. The time we would typically use to fulfilling our fleshly desires would better be spent in building our faith in God.

Think about it and determine which one will prepare you for what it is you say you want, which is marriage. Dating allows you to share yourself over and again with those who treat you as the current flavor of the month. Courting allows you to prepare yourself for the one who will honor you as God's divine best.

Zamaya's Testimony

How "A Good Thing To Be Found Helped Me."

    I was on the fence about a relationship that I was in. He was a minister of music. This meant he was holy, set apart, and filled with the Holy Spirit, right? Wrong! Real wrong. I thought he was the one. In fact, he was the one! The very one that would try to assassinate the very character of a true godly man. Would it not be just like Satan to try to promote the agenda that a good man is hard to find. However, I will not blame him entirely. I was wrong too. And to say that by allowing him to touch me in any fashion didn't assassinate the character of godly women? I can only pray not. Beginning at the age of 13, I can say that I have had two very strong convictions: The first, I love God with all my being, and second, what God has for me is for me. I tried to walk in a way I thought was pleasing to God. However, some of what I believed was tainted by what the world promoted. Dating seemed like a natural activity of life. It was like a part of the grand scheme of things. I just knew it fit in my picture! This had to be God's will, right? Everybody's doing it. I wouldn't be wrong, right? How else will I fall in love and live the American Dream? The Lord has greater plans for me. He has an amazing Boaz somewhere being groomed just for me. However, God needed me, the Ruth, to be in the right field at the right time. The right field and the right time required that I be whole: mind, body and soul. God sent me to a marriage preparation class called, "A Good Thing To Be Found" hosted by the amazing Mamie Fay Walton. Mrs. Walton smiled when you entered her class. She even asked you how you were doing. After the pleasantries came the mirror. This wasn't the kind of mirror that you look into and see that every hair is in place, or that you have well designed your outfit. This mirror reflected the very heart of you. Your every thought of who you were and how you arrived at that point, surfaced. The good, the bad, and all the ugly stood as if to expose you. It was almost as if you were naked. I was not ashamed. I learned that in spite of my past and because of the hope of my future, I am "A Good Thing to be Found." I am not a rummage sale where you just pick all over me. I am not a yard sale where someone has decided to get rid of me because I am no longer of use. There is a price on my life but I am not for sale. I have already been purchased by a Risen Savior. No, I did not have a lot of women around me to show me how to become a Proverbs 31 woman. This class gave me the foundation I needed to become one. And that is just what I am doing, four years later, Becoming. There are no doubts that when my Boaz comes, he will call Mrs. Walton and say, "Thank you, for helping her to become, "A Good Thing I Could Find".

Zamaya

Get Yourself Together: Cooking

Need I say more? You're back from your two week honeymoon where you have eaten out each day. The luggage is dropped just inside the door. Your husband is tired: Tired of airports, crowds, driving, and buffets. The next thing he says as he plops down onto the leather couch is, "What can you cook up in a hurry?" You almost go into cardiac arrest, because you knew this day would come. You didn't anticipate it arriving so quickly. Since you never got to be a part of one of my classes, you didn't make learning how to cook quick meals a priority. You thought you would be fine since there are fast food restaurants that stay open until one in the morning. There is a saying that states that the way to a man's heart is through his stomach. Well, that didn't change when he received Christ. The man wants to eat! You have to be able to deliver. What's a girl to do in preparation for the next level of marriage? There are many things you can do, which you will see when you take my online course. Until then, go to Google and do a search for easy recipes. You will be surprised at what you will find. Then, try a new recipe a week. Print it out and begin to create a file of easy recipes for breakfast, lunch and dinner, and even appetizers. Girl, before you know it, you will not only love being in the kitchen, you will know what you are doing, too. You go girl! I can smell that casserole and almost taste those greens. No more TV dinners for you. Get yourself together.

-3-

Bees Are Drawn To Honey: What Is Drawn To You?

Take a moment to look back over your years of dating and consider the type of men you attracted. What characteristics does each one have in common? Take another moment to consider each one and write down the first three things that come to your mind.

Here are two examples: Romeo with big ears, steel wool hair and six toes on one foot or Romeo who is quick tempered, verbally abusive and stingy.

The first example is not a good one because you are basing your decisions on the way "Romeo" looks. Physical appearance should not be up for discussion. "Romeo" cannot help the way he was created, at least not without spending thousands of dollars. It is not right or fair to pass judgment on a person for the way that he or she was created. It is also unwise to look down on another person and deem them to be unworthy of your presence because of something as shallow as the size of their ears.

If you wrote a list similar to the second example, then you are on the right path.

It is a good example because these are issues that speak to a person's character. Again, you don't want to look down on someone because there is an area in his or her life that needs to be yielded to God. Remember, we all need some work.

When you have completed making your lists circle all of the characteristics that each guy has in common. In doing so, you should be able to find multiple similarities. These are similarities that are ultimately drawn to you. In other words, you attract who you are or how you feel about yourself.

To help you better understand where I am going with this, I'll give another example. Let's say that you recognize that almost all of your past boyfriends were verbally abusive; that several of them have even pushed you around. What is it in you that you have allowed such behavior and treatment? Men who have this issue will seek out women who lack self-confidence. They usually have no dealings with women who are sure of themselves.

This little exercise was designed to help you to recognize the type of men you attract. If you don't like the type of men you are attracting, then it's time to do a self-assessment and make some changes. In order to make those changes, you would first need to learn who you are in Christ. When you know who you are and what you are destined to become in HIM, you will cease from attracting men like "Romeo".

Remember, you will one day marry what you are attracting. If you are constantly attracting someone like "Romeo," your marriage will be set up for disaster.

Know Who You Are

Does a uniformed security guard have the authority to tell a uniformed police officer to put down his weapon and put his hands where he can see them? No. Would an officer obey such a command? No, because he knows who he is.

If we take time to find out who we are in Christ, no one could ever devalue us again. We become empowered when we know who we are. Unfortunately, so many of us spend little time in communion with God to develop our relationship with Him. In doing so, we inadvertently give the enemy room to work in our lives. We have weapons that possess amazing spiritual powers. If we do not spend time with God to learn how to wield and yield those weapons, Satan, our enemy, can and often does use those very same weapons against us. Remember, it's not enough to know that you have weapons; you also have to know how to work them. When you are in communion with God, you can hear from God clearer. He speaks in different ways. We just have to have an ear to hear what the spirit is saying.

Not knowing who we are can cause us to live beneath our birth rites. Everything that we settle for will eventually reflect back into our lives, including who we settled for in a man. We will begin to say things like, "I know he's not born again, but God showed me him preaching the word. So I know that we will get there one day. It is just a matter of time."

A good example of this is when, a few years ago before I met my husband, a man, who was trying to get me to date him, told of a time when he broke his sister's jaw (this was before he came to Christ). As he related the story to me, I began to listen intently to his heart to see if I could hear any words of remorse or repentance for what he had done. There were none. When I brought this to his attention, he responded by stating that his sister should have never gotten in his face "like that."

I already knew that he was not God's divine best for me. If I had any questions in my mind about it up to that point, he had just answered it. The answer was, NO WAY! Besides, I like my jaw the way it is. The minute he let his guard down, his heart began to speak and I heard it loud and clear.

It is important to have a relationship with God in order to get to know who you are in Him. Here is a story of a guy who once told me that "back in the day" he had girls who used to fall over him who would do anything he wanted them to do. He was trying to get me to go out with him and I wouldn't. His comment to me was, "I could have any girl I want at church, but I choose you, and I can't even get you out on a date."

Thank God I was able to see through his trickery. He first started out by pumping himself up when he bragged about all the girls he was able to get "back in the day," and he went on to compare me to those women. That wasn't enough. He went on to try to make me feel privileged that out of all the women at the church he could have, he considered me. "Get real buddy." There were several spirits operating within this dialogue; one of them was the Spirit of Control. This guy tried hard to manipulate me with his words. He wanted to devalue me so that I would put him on a pedestal and view him to be of greater value than myself. He wanted me to submit to the desires of his impure heart. If I had not taken the time to get to know who I was in Christ, he may have succeeded. I did know who I was and I let him know it. Can you imagine what my response was? No, I didn't blast the poor guy. I certainly did not let him off easy, either. I responded by saying, "I don't care what you say other women did to you or for you. I am a consecrated servant of God walking in integrity. I've been kept by the power of God. I am a rare species as you have never encountered before. A virgin waiting on God's best and you are not it! You ought to be honored that I gave you a portion of my time. You're skipping around the church looking for who you can devour, but you have been exposed. You need to repent. Now would be a good time." I also encouraged him to not allow the enemy to use him to destroy or even harm the women of God in any way.

I can imagine that some of you may feel that I was a little harsh. Please understand that I was not dealing with him, but rather the spirit that was influencing him. During the conversation, the Spirit of God had already showed me that this guy had used this same line on many other Christian women., Had I not known who I was in Christ, I may have entertained him just like the other women. When we have no idea of the power we have, it gives Satan the opportunity to take advantage of us. Get in the word!

I urge you to search to see what the word of God says about who you truly are in Christ. To make things a little easier for you, I took liberty of providing you with something that you can turn into a daily confession to build your confidence in Christ even more. I encourage you to make these confessions a part of your daily living:

- I AM saved by God's grace (Ephesians 2:5)
- I AM blessed with all spiritual blessings in heavenly places in Christ (Ephesians 1:3).
- I AM holy without blame (Ephesians 1:4).
- I AM accepted in the beloved (Ephesians 1:6).
- I AM redeemed through the blood of Jesus (Ephesians 1:7).
- I AM a person of wisdom and prudence (Ephesians 1:8).
- I AM an heir (Ephesians 1:11).
- I AM seated in heavenly places in Christ Jesus (Ephesians 2:6).
- I AM near to God by the blood of Christ (Ephesians 2:13).
- I AM a new creation (Ephesians 2:15).
- I AM a citizen of heaven (Ephesians 2:19).
- I AM a partaker of His promises in Christ (2 Peter 1:4).
- I AM strengthened with might through His spirit (Ephesians 3:16).

- I AM rooted and grounded in love (Ephesians 3:17).
- I AM rooted in the spirit of my mind (Ephesians 4:23).
- I AM filled with the spirit (Ephesians 5:18).
- I AM more than a conqueror (Romans 8:31).
- I AM an overcomer (Revelation 12:11).
- I AM His righteousness in Christ Jesus (I Corinthians 1:30).
- I AM healed (I Peter 2:24).
- I AM consecrated (Corinthians 6:11).
- I AM crucified (I Corinthians 6:11).
- I AM victorious (1 John 5:4).
- I AM free (John 8:36).

As you read these scriptures, you may have thought to yourself, "That's not me. I'm not there yet." If that is how you feel, ask the Lord to show you how these words can be manifested in your life. Say them daily with feeling and conviction. The demons walking this earth know who you are and now you do too. Shout out loud, "I AM!"

Sometimes there are no short cuts to what we need to do. We just have to do it. We must know and be confident in who we are so we don't settle for a counterfeit of God's divine best. Everything about you should attract a godly man and not the same old, same old. Aren't you ready for a change?

If you are not, you may have already considered throwing this book aside, calling your boyfriend to complain about what you have read. You cannot stand the thought of not having a man in your life who will spend money on you and romance you with candlelight dinners.

Have you ever thought about cultivating your relationship with the Lord instead? God is just waiting for you to express your love for Him. You often overlook spending time in His word of prayer to hear what He has to say. You prefer to seek out or cultivate a relationship that is not for you. I tell you the truth, there is life after dating. Imagine a child who is used to going trick or treating for Halloween. His parents, now born again, have gained a better understanding of the true meaning behind Halloween and no longer allow their child to engage in the celebration of that day. The child, who had become accustomed to going shopping for costumes (often dressing up as Satan with horns and a tail) is now no longer permitted to partake in the festivities. What will become of this poor child who is made to suffer change due to the decision his parents made as a result of their desire to walk closer with the Lord? He'll adjust! So will you.

You have a host of witnesses, including yourself, that can attest to the conflicts encountered when believers date outside of the will of God. One trick of the enemy is to try and tempt us into getting into relationships that are no good for us. They attempt to keep us out of the presence of God. Instead of taking time to get to know God, and get to know who we are in God in preparation for marriage, we will instead spend this valuable time with a man. Starting a relationship that we knew was not ours from the beginning.

Men of God will never hold us in high esteem until we begin to hold ourselves in high esteem. We must incorporate higher standard into our lives. One such standard would be to announce that you are neither for rent nor for lease. You will not be some man's part-time lover. You are under reconstruction by God in preparation for marriage. Are you doing this? No, but you should.

There is so much work to be done in advancing the kingdom. We just do not have time to waste stroking our flesh or allowing our flesh to be soothed. Our adversary, the Devil, is on a mission and we should be too! Let our cry be, "God, send our spouses our way! Men who we can truly share ourselves with in the presence of God. Give us a relationship. Give us a covenant that honors Christ and is ordained by God."

It is possible to go from singleness to marriage without being a girlfriend first. You are probably wondering to yourself, "How will I get to know a guy if I don't date him first?" Well, I'll tell you. Reading this book is a start. But your first step should be in asking God to remake you as a woman of God in preparation for marriage. When God deems you ready for presentation, allow Him to do just that—present you. By the time you are ready to be presented, God would have already spoken to the man's heart confirming you are the one he has been seeking. The Spirit of God in you will bear witness to this. The man God has chosen to be your husband will make known his intentions. After you have prayed, fasted and consulted with parents and your spiritual mentor, the two of you will begin to spend time together in a God-honoring way with the intent to marry.

Now, while God is working on you, ask Him to sharpen your spirit of discernment.

My Testimony

One day, while at my friend Tamera's house cat sitting her rather large sick feline "Biggums", I sat down and began to think about my singleness, and my life as a whole. I came to a shocking conclusion. I had maximized my singleness as a believer. There wasn't much else I could do within the scope of my calling besides what I had already been doing. What a sobering moment. Then I said something to the Lord I think I will always remember. I said, "Lord, I think I am ready for companionship." In the past, this was not even a thought in my mind because I had truly become content in my singleness. Just then the spirit of God took me away in a vision to a room that was black like a chalk board. It felt like time travel. I stood in a gown while across from me was a man in a tuxedo and white gloves. He leaned over to kiss me. When he did a thick white chalk line appeared between us. He backed up and said, "No, not yet." The spirit of the Lord spoke to me in my vision. He told me to fast so that He could remake me as a woman of God. He also said He would reveal who my husband was if I remained faithful and focused to the fast. Just like that, the vision was over. All I could remember was the Lord wanted me to stay faithful and focused. The rest I could not recall. I shared with no one else what I shared with God that day. This one was between God and me and no one else. From that day on, the Lord began changing me from the inside out. I embraced the changes and in the process God made me a "Good Thing to Be Found!"

One of the things I did during this six-month fasting period was to immediately change my seating at church. Instead of sitting in the back of the church, I took a new seat in the front row. If I had to come to church one hour earlier to get that seat, then I did. The move helped to keep me focused on the Word and not all the single men coming in the door. Sitting in the front delivered me from the distractions of the opposite sex that robbed my devotions from more godly attractions. I was able to spend more time in the Word. I also stopped individual fellowship with men of God to stay focused on the things of God.

One night during my time of fasting, the Lord woke me up around 2 o'clock in the morning to pray. I have to admit that I don't usually awaken at that ungodly hour. I did what most of you Bible-believing Christians would have done. I dropped to my knees and fell asleep. Before I could get into a good dream, the Lord would wake me again to pray. After God and I went through this whole "wake-up to fall asleep while praying thing," I stood up from kneeling and told God he was God so he knew why he was calling me to prayer. I told him to tell me what he needed me to pray. Then I could pray and get back to sleep again. After a moment of silence, I said, "I know: Levelle. Tell me why he's in my life." From that moment, 2:30 a.m. until a little after 12 that afternoon, I could hear

God answering the question that I had asked Him. God said, "You know who he is. You'll know who he is when you look into his eyes." If this had happened to you, I know that by 12 noon you would have called twenty of your closest girlfriends to share the good news. Wisdom told me, however, to keep it to myself. Single women, if you feel that the spirit has revealed your mate to you I would kindly offer this bit of advice: KEEP YOUR MOUTH SHUT! Maintain your integrity for God's sake. You never want to share a word prematurely.

Later on that evening, my roommates and I were relaxing at home when Levelle's roommate stopped by to share with us that Levelle had heard from God about his wife that morning around 2:30. Levelle wasn't telling anyone until he had a chance to tell her. What do you think I was thinking about at that time? My heart was doing flips! But I still managed to stand still and be quiet.

I told not a soul about my experience. I didn't want word to get back to Levelle and risk tainting or swaying his heart from me. Too often we have rushed to share what God has spoken concerning the man He has chosen. Then the man of God becomes confused and wonders why God didn't tell him. Wait and let the man of God find you for a change.

That evening at church, and before New Year's Eve service began, Levelle pulled me aside and told me that he was up late the night before praying about his wife. He said that God had directed him to Proverbs 31 and asked Levelle to compare it to women of God that he knew. Levelle reported to the

Lord that none of the women lined up. Then, God said to him, "Now try Fay." Levelle did, and I lined up perfectly. The Lord then told Levelle that he had found his wife. The rest is history! Would you like to guess what day this all took place on? The day that my fast was over, the same day that the Lord told me he would reveal who my husband was. I had been faithful and focused and God was faithful to his word.

Am I any better than you? I think you know that answer. You can do it. Take yourself off the "available to be your girlfriend auction block" and use that time to spend quality time in the presence of God. Doing so will maximize your spiritual singleness. Ask God to remake you as a woman of God to be more effective in the kingdom. This will complete your preparation for the next level which is marriage.

Chandra's Testimony

What does a "Good Thing to be Found" mean?

"A Good Thing to be Found" takes its name from Proverbs 18:22 which states:

"Whoso findeth a wife findeth a good thing, and obtaineth favour of the Lord" (King James Version Bible.)

This means: "Stop being THIRSTY. Stop being DESPERATE. Stop SETTLING. Stop looking at every man that approaches you as "The One!" Ninety-nine percent of the time, he AIN'T!!"

Marriage preparation classes have taught me to seek God first and not worry about when a man will come. The classes have taught me to go after God with my whole heart so that **He** can repair and mend it! These classes were nothing short of TRANSFORMATIVE! They were designed to be a two-part series. While studying, I learned so much about the Word, myself, and how men view women that I went through three parts! At times, the classes were an uncomfortable mirror and I couldn't wait to get out of the sessions, especially the "Get Yourself Together" segments! I dreaded those sessions because it was painfully obvious that I had, and still have, so much work to do on myself before I could even begin to think about bringing someone else into my life.

In other sessions, I was so enthralled with the teachings that I hated for them to end! These classes were life changing. Not only did they deal with what the Bible says about marriage and dating (it's not in there!) The studies talked about soul ties, premarital sex, masturbation, accountability, and how to be a woman. In these classes, we also discussed the importance of keeping our cars clean and learning how to change tires and check the air pressure. We shared recipes, discussed what to do during a certain time of the month, and what it means for us when our hearts are passed around from person to person.

There were several lessons that impacted me the most, and those lessons were:

#1 – "Get Yourself Together!" segments
#2 – "Be Faithful & Focused!"

#3 – "Maximize Your Singleness!"
#4 – The True Definition of "Girlfriend" is FLAVOR OF THE MONTH. Don't be one!

Ultimately, discover your passions and purposes and go after them. Do everything you've desired to do. Go back to school, travel, learn to cook, find a new hobby, lose weight, get your finances in order, and even change your hair color and style if you want.

But most importantly, "Get off the island and get an accountability partner." Find someone who loves you enough to ask hard, uncomfortable questions. I still struggle with this one but it's one of the most important things I've learned about myself: I need accountability. I can't live without it.

These classes have left me with the best spiritual and adopted parents in the world! There are none like the Waltons anywhere. During the time I was taking the first class, I was going through a period of malcontent with my birth mother and Mama Fay became my mother. I don't have a great relationship with my birth father and Daddy Levelle has become my father. He doesn't know it but I want him to walk me down the aisle. (I'm praying for my future husband as I type this because he's going to have to meet all of my parents!) These classes have ruined me in a good way and I am now unable to act as I once did, in a carnal way. When those moments arise, I hear Mama Fay's voice.

When I'm procrastinating or being lazy, or watching too much television, as I'm known to do, I hear Mom again: "Be faithful and focused…get involved at church…maximize your singleness… get up and do something!"

When I am busy at my pity party for one, lamenting on lost time, missed dreams, broken promises, and untapped potential, Mom says, "And who knoweth whether thou art come to the kingdom for such a time as this?" Esther 4:14b (KJV). What she is saying is to "Redeem the time…better yourself…stop living in the past…your journey has prepared you for this very moment! God is your future…Go after HIM!"

Marriage preparation is training through courses, seminars, or counseling that prepares for a successful marriage. With the high divorce rate among believers, it is imperative that we as Christians train and equip ourselves as singles so that we can work to lay a godly foundation to our marriage and be the example that the Bible speaks about and not the statistic the world points to. Some of the most serious challenges that most couples face are: Balancing job and family; frequency of sexual relations; debt brought into marriage; separate bank accounts and other finances; employment difficulties; expectations about household tasks and other gender roles; communication; problematic parents or in-laws; lack of time spent together; and differences in parenting styles. This class goes through all of those issues and uses "What Would You Do?" and "How Would You Respond?" scenarios to highlight the areas where we need strengthening or where we can be a pillar for others. The classes are fun, informative, introspective, and an invaluable building tool worth any dollar amount that is attached to it! There's not a day that goes by that I don't recall something that was taught in that class. I would get so excited about the preparations that God had me going through that I would bring those lessons back home to friends and family members, even if they, at the time, did not or could not understand. I now often hear one of them say, "Hey! Didn't you learn that in marriage preparation class?" Being able to impart a truth like that to others as it was given to me has no price tag. I will never be the same.

Chandra

Get Yourself Together: Cleanliness Is Next To Godliness: Part 1

I don't know how true that old adage is, but if you ask me, they ran out of ink when printing the Bible, so it was left out. In my opinion, it should have made it in there. Can I be real with you since it's just you and me talking right now?

There is a chance that you could be the one for him, but God forbid if he should see your car before he hears from God about you. You know, the one full of papers and trash and God only knows what that is growing in the grimy carpet? Yeah, that. If he sees your filthy car, he will be confident you are not the one. Have you ever passed a sign that reads "Car Wash?" Put that dirty nasty thing in reverse, go back one block and turn in. The sign calls out to you, "Girl, clean that thing!"

Lord give me a man!

A friend gave me a ride to church once and I had worn a white suit that day. I climbed into her cluttered car and away we went. It was not until we got to church and I attempted to get out of her car that I failed to notice the candy stuck to her seat. When I attempted to get out of the vehicle, my skirt was stuck to the seat, stuck to a piece of old candy. It was hot and I guess the heat made the candy melt which made it sticky. I also had a French fry stuck to my behind and here we are at church and in a hurry. You can imagine it was hard for me to worship with French fry grease and orange sticky candy stains on my behind. If cleanliness is next to Godliness, then someone's in trouble. Get yourself together. Get yourself together!

Affirmation: I refuse to allow unidentifiable things to grow in the carpet or fibers of my vehicle's seats, because I'm not nasty. Please read aloud if possible 3 times.

-4-

A Good Thing To Be <u>Found</u>

Squeak! went the church doors during service and enters in a visitor, a man. As he walks down the aisle in search of a seat, he passes your row and you grab a quick glimpse of his face, his muscles, and finally that butt. Yeah, I said it, that butt. You do not want to admit it, but you cannot even count the times you have checked men out in this way. The Bible tells us that every man and woman in Christ is our brother and sister. That idea alone should cause you to put an end to such behavior. That may also be another reason why we should not look to one another for dating purposes. You would not date your brother or sister, would you? Often, women find themselves pursuing men. That is fine for the world, but once again, we bring it into the church. When are we going to leave the ways of the world alone?

Women were never designed to pursue but rather to be pursued. It is no secret that man, by nature, is a hunter. In many different ways they hunt for what it is they want. They enjoy the hunt because the main purpose of hunting is to conquer. When we pursue the man and engage in the sport of hunting or fishing, we remove their opportunity to be who they were designed to be. Most men do not feel successful if you lay a thing at their feet. They would much rather have testimonies on how they pursued and obtained what they were after.

Imagine this. A man pays for his hunting license, takes two days off away from work and family to spend time with the guys. This is the year he is going to bag that buck. At this point, all the other guys have gotten their deer and the weekend is hours away from being over. He spots the largest one of the season and can taste it. It is his! He aims, waiting for the eight-point and just before he shoots, his buddy, who has already bagged his deer but feels sorry for his friend, shoots the deer, and hooks him clean off of his feet. He proceeds to drag the stag over to his friend and says, "It's all yours." How do you think that man feels? Do you believe he was grateful to his friend for saving him from the embarrassment of having been the only one not to bag a deer? No! What his buddy intentionally did was shame him. He also took away his story. Every man likes to tell the story.

Ladies, the word of God says that, "He who finds a wife, finds a good thing and obtains favor from the Lord." This scripture alone tells us that the man does the looking, not the woman. Perhaps, it is because of the whole "man being the hunter" thing. I do not know. What I do know, is that the word of God is the word of God, and we can continue to go against it if we want; there is always a price to pay for doing so.

Recently, a young man was asked why he had not been seen at church in quite some time. He replied that every time he turned around "one of the single women would tell me that she had heard from God about me and that I was her husband. I got fed up with it and I left the fellowship. I still worship the Lord, just not there."

Another gentleman visited a church. After a few Sundays, he is approached by a young lady who had actually ushered him to his seat every time he visited. She also claimed that God had spoken to her and said, "There goes your husband." The young lady was adamant that she heard the words while ushering him to his seat. She said, "I am convinced you are to be my husband and I want to know you better." The gentleman takes a deep breath and replies, "I hope that I have not given you an impression that I was interested in you. You see, I am happily married to my wife of twenty-one years. She has just had a stroke and cannot attend church with me. I was visiting your church because I saw your pastor on television and I was blessed." The woman, totally embarrassed, became bitter with God. She felt God had set her up to be hurt. She decided she could never serve a God who could be so cruel. She has left the church and wants nothing to do with God.

What went wrong? Ladies, hear me well. If by any chance you feel the Lord has spoken to you regarding a particular man being your husband, keep your mouth shut! Stay in communication with God about the word you feel you have received. And do not lose your faith or focus. In my testimony, I shared with you that I had not shared with anyone God's revelation to me about who my husband was. Later, I found out that several women had approached Levelle during the beginning of his walk with the Lord, proclaiming God said he was their husband. Can you imagine how great a stumbling block that became for him during his early walk with God? If we are not careful, we can operate in trickery. When we go ahead of God and share such information, information that the man knows is wrong but entertains anyway because of his immaturity in God, he is swayed into believing that you heard correctly. This is trickery.

In this instance, trickery would be using the name or even the influence of God to get another to do what you want them to do or to go along with how you see a thing or what you desire a thing to be.

In essence, you spot a man who is new in his faith and walk with the Lord and tell him you heard the Lord say he was to be your husband. Because he believes you have been in Christ longer than he, he may lean on what he thinks is your ability to hear from the Lord and now you have successfully engaged in trickery. God is not pleased! No more fishing for men! God has someone specifically designed for you. Will you be ready when he presents himself?

Stop Looking Hungry!

You probably think this is related to food somehow. However, it's not. This is for the single women who are not satisfied with being single. They have a certain look about them that a man terms as being, "hungry." Just as a shark can smell blood, so can a man—born again or not— detect a hungry woman.

Men know that one of the best places to find a hungry woman is at a wedding. Ladies, it's good to go to weddings but if you aren't content with being a single woman, then I suggest that when you get that pretty invitation in the mail (you know the one with the two doves enclosed in a heart, kissing), check the "unable to attend" box on the invitation response card and ask God to teach you the benefits of being single until you become content with it.

Women take in everything at weddings. Not a lot gets past us because we long to be married. We develop a look that says, "I wish that were me" or "Lord, when is my day going to come?" that men pick up on. That's why single men know that weddings are the hottest spots to pick up women.

A man attends a wedding with an invitation in hand. He attends to show his support and to look for someone who looks hungry for a relationship. It doesn't take long before he spots her. He knew she was available because throughout the ceremony she had that, "By this time next year, I'm going to have me a man too" look on her face. After the ceremony, the prowler introduces himself and quickly learns that the woman is headed to the reception. He tells her to save a dance for him. They end up dancing every chance they got and began to date after that night. He was always the perfect gentleman, taking her to expensive restaurants and showering her with gifts. He never seemed to want anything in return. "Too good to be true," her girlfriends tell her. He even went to church with her several times. Then he pops the question. With tears in her eyes she replies, "Yes, I will marry you." The carats he placed on her finger were so great they made a rabbit sit up and take notice. Weeks before the wedding and over dinner, she begins to joyfully talk about what their life will be like together. As that rock on her ring finger nearly blinded all who passed by, he said, "Let's just clarify a few things up front. You can have whatever you want; money is not a problem. We will live together but have separate rooms. You live your life and I will live mine. We must go to visit our families on holidays for appearances sake and for God sakes don't even plan on children, I don't want any."

By now, you've guessed it. He was living a homosexual life and due to pressure from his family (who didn't know about his lifestyle) to marry, he went to the wedding looking for Ms. Lord, give me a man! and he found her. How embarrassed she must have been to have to tell her friends and family that the engagement was off. Remember ladies, if you don't look hungry, guys will stop trying to feed you mess. So, before you go to a wedding, check your motive, your heart, and "get yourself together!"

Affirmation: "I am going to allow God to make me a whole woman of God so that when I am out I don't appear as if I am looking for someone to complete me. God is enough!"

Lord, Please Don't Bend Over

One thing single sober minded Christian men don't like is the way Christian women use worldly tactics to snag a man of God. You don't need to snag a man. When the wife is ready the husband will come. You have so much you could be doing than leaving the top two buttons of your blouse open; wearing pants that refuse to allow your pores to exhale; and wearing skirts shorter than a pull up diaper. Focus on your life in Christ, focus on going higher in God, and focus on your faithfulness to God and His kingdom business. Be a blessing to your local church. They need your gifts in some area of the church.

There was a woman at a church I once attended who had a habit of wearing short, short skirts, the kind that don't permit you to bend over in any kind of way. One day after service, my husband and I were finishing up a conversation with another couple, and she spoke to me. Just then I dropped my program and she nearly dropped her bible notebook and CD of the morning message to bend over to get my program for me. The first thing that came out of my mouth was, "I know you're not going to bend over and get that." She stopped in her tracks as my fingers grabbed hold of the paper. Clearly, I was the best candidate to play pick up in the presence of my husband. She got the message. However, my husband had just turned as my paper fell. He neither saw her rescue attempt

Lord give me a man!

nor heard her response. Later, she apologized. She knew she was wrong. I apologized if I hurt her feelings. That was not my intent.

Ladies, let's not do things to attract a guy's attention. Again, when the wife is ready, the husband will appear. Are you ready? On purpose or not, some things that women do to attract a man of God can be a stumbling. Some women feel justified in stating, "They shouldn't look." I say, "If it's not for sale, take the sign down." Don't advertise the body parts that should be covered. When you put on a blouse, start with the top button. Consult the Holy Spirit prior to making purchases to assure what you wear is not offending the heart of God. Ladies, if you have a little extra breast, then please wear a bra that will keep your girls held in. Truth be told, sometimes your cup runs over. This is not attractive, rather a turn off. If you don't know what your true size is (most of us think we do but we don't), go to a good department store and ask to be measured, and then purchase accordingly.

Now, let's head on down to the cake aisle. Girls, we can do better when it comes to our panties. Yeah, I am going to say it: If you must wear those uncomfortable strands of material separating your cakes, called thongs, please make sure that your pants or skirts are not a transparent color or material. In the church, the man of God does not need to change seats just to enter the presence of God because you have on a thong that is visible through your off white pants. Some of us are wearing thongs when we need to be wearing a girdle. Take off the thong and get a girdle on, now. This will prevent the avalanche that takes place when you are standing one seat in front of a man (who the bible calls your brother) shaking and clapping. Ladies, what's a man to do? Just Stop Tempting a Brother and "get yourself together!"

Affirmation: I will not be the cause of the man of God's struggle. Lord, show me what's in my wardrobe that shouldn't be.

Get Yourself Together!: Cleanliness Is Next To Godliness: Part II

It is a known fact that when you sit on a person's toilet, you can tell how clean they are. Think about it. When you walk into a person's bathroom, it may appear clean, but while you are on the toilet (without a magazine), you get a chance to look at things a little closer. When I was at a gathering at Levelle's house, before we were engaged, I used his bathroom. The pilgrimage from the front door to the bathroom was one of the neatest experiences I had ever had. His house was literally one of the neatest, tidiest homes I had ever been in that was owned by a man. As I entered the bathroom and began to walk on the marble floors, I was really in awe. But it wasn't until my legs were swinging over that toilet, that I realized how clean the man really was. The base of the tub was toothbrush clean and the toilet as well. Windows and window seals as well. Towels were fresh and clean; all brass fixtures without scum or even water spots. The whirl pool was spotless. It was then that I said to myself, "Either this man is clean or he has a housekeeper he should never fire." Come to find out, his entire home was just like his bathroom. How about you? What will a person gather about you as their feet swing from your toilet? Get on a house cleaning schedule so your home can be clean. Does your home have an old stale odor to it when you enter? Is it cluttered and dusty? If someone were to open your refrigerator, would mold greet them? Are there ketchup drippings on the door? Develop a system. Certain things like dusting and cleaning windows are done on Friday. Floors and laundry are done Saturday morning, etc. If you know that on Saturday you will be away from home, double up on Friday. Bottom line is: "get yourself together!"

Affirmation: I have always owned a mop, a rag, and a bucket, but today I bring them out of retirement.

Jandalyn's Testimony: Marriage Preparation

In order to have a fulfilling married life, you must have a successful single life. Divorce is running rampant in the Church and this is due to poor preparation during singlehood. In Matthew 25, Jesus tells the parable of the ten virgins. Five were wise and with forethought, and the other five were foolish. They were all waiting to see the bridegroom. When the bridegroom was slow in coming, they all fell asleep. All of a sudden, the bridegroom showed up, and the ten virgins got up to put their lamps in order. The wise had oil in their lamps while the foolish did not. In fact, the foolish asked that the wise virgins give them some of their oil. The wise refused to do so. The foolish virgins had to go into town to purchase the oil to fill their lamps. Meanwhile the wise virgins were fellowshipping with the bridegroom. When the foolish virgins arrived, they were not permitted to go in to the banquet because the bridegroom did not recognize them, even though the foolish were expecting to go in to see him. Maybe the bridegroom was harsh in his dealings with the foolish virgins, and maybe not. The point is that the virgins that were prepared were permitted to see their groom. This is the state of the church today. We want the blessings of God but we do not factor in the preparation that is needed to maintain the blessing.

When it comes to marriage preparation, we can no longer remain in ignorance about what God expects from us as believers. We must apply the mind of Christ as we journey from singlehood to marriage. First of all, Christ is love. The love walk must be our highest aspiration, our great quest (1 Corinthians 13:4-8 Amplified Bible). It is vital that we allow God to mature us in this area, especially during our single years. This is called spiritual preparation. For example, I live with my dad and my younger brother. God is teaching me to love my brother just the way he is and refrain from nagging him to get what I want from him. I am learning the art of praising a man in order to build his spirit man so that he can fulfill the call of God on his life. Then there is natural preparation. This includes keeping the house clean, managing money correctly, and fulfilling educational goals so that when I get married, I can devote my life to being a wife and a mother to our children.

It took me a very long time for me to come to these conclusions. In the beginning, I was so desperate to marry, I thought every man that came into my path was a potential husband. I looked at merely the physical side of a man, how good looking he was, and totally neglected the spiritual. In those days, my flesh was completely dominating my life. I wanted to marry just so I could have sex; to spend it on fleshly desires. God began to teach me that He wanted me married, however I was going about it the wrong way. This brought hope to me because I was under the deception that you can't be sure if God wants you married in the first place. Well if that were true, then there would be no need for preparation. Think about it: God prepared Jesus before the foundation of the world. Jesus Himself went away to prepare a place for us. Noah prepared an ark for the flood that was to come.

Satan is attacking the Church concerning marriage. You have singles confused as to whether or not God wants them married or not and homosexuals fighting for the right to marry. The fact of the matter is that God established marriage in the beginning and marriage will be fulfilled in the end. True biblical marriage will always be between man and woman. God's intention is that He wanted man and woman to be fruitful and multiply, to replenish the earth with godly people and children (Genesis 1:26-28). Our Lord gave us this commandment once more in Noah's account. He told Noah to be fruitful and multiply.

Several years ago, the Lord allowed me to meet a couple who lived this life of preparation during singlehood before they got married. Fay Walton taught classes for single women titled, "A Good Thing to be Found." I attended these classes and found out that the very thing God was trying to teach me was being confirmed in these classes. The teachings completely solidified what the Lord was doing within me. We talked about many topics, ranging from forgiveness to culinary classes to financial preparedness. Fay taught us the day to day operations of running a household and putting her husband's needs first with God having preeminence. This is just a small synopsis of the many, many things I learned from this woman of God. Levelle, her husband, showed us ways that we could keep ourselves healthy, and gave us insight on what makes men tick. Since attending their classes, I am amazed at the fact of how I am still walking out the preparation steps that were taught to me all those years ago. I was in my early thirty's when I started on this journey. I will be forty years old this year and I can truly say if it wasn't for Fay and Levelle's teaching, I would be far behind spiritually and naturally. I can say with confidence that when, not if, but when I marry, I will be totally prepared. God will definitely get the glory in our marriage. This is due to the seed of preparation planted in me by Mamie and Levelle Walton.

-5-
Accountability

Think about all of those who are your friends, family, and associates. Out of all of those people, who is it that you are accountable to? Who is it that knows the true you? Is that person someone who helps keep you on track spiritually and in other areas of your life?

Every believer needs someone in their life with whom they are accountable. This person should be someone you have gone to and asked if you could be accountable to them. You would call them on a consistent basis to discuss where you are in your spiritual walk as it pertains to your prayer life, fasting, tithing, forgiveness, love walk, and other areas of your life. This person, in turn, will be able to, and should be able to, ask you the hard questions that will help to keep you on track.

Some examples of hard questions that they may ask and the ones that I may use are the following:

1) If your love for God was reflected by how much time you spent with Him this past week, how would you rate it on a scale from 1 to 10?
2) You said that you use to have a problem with pornography and we know that the word of God encourages us to set no wicked thing before us (Psalms 101:3). How do you feel God would rate you in this area now? Are there any problems in this area that you need prayer in?
3) You may have told me in a prior conversation that being seventy pounds overweight was affecting your breathing. What exactly are your plans to correct that?
4) For the past seven months, you have been working on your budget in an effort to get out of debt. I need you to call me the on the first of next month with your budget completed so that we can go over it together. you must be serious about working on your finances.

Your Accountability Partner is not your buddy, your girl, or your under paid servant. What she is, is godly help sent by God to help get you and then keep you on the straight and narrow path. She is also in place to help keep you in a place where God is being glorified in your life. How can you tell if you have the wrong partner, you may ask? I can give you two things to consider: If a godly woman has a man for an accountability partner, then he is the wrong partner. Also, if your partner is struggling in her flesh then she is the wrong partner.

No Fancy Footwear Needed!

Your accountability partner should not need expensive footwear in an attempt to catch up with you. It is your job to pray and ask God to direct you to a person with whom you can be truly accountable. It is your job to submit to authority and to stay in contact with them, to touch bases with them, share growth, and seek counsel. Without some sort of accountability, you are almost out there on your own. You could be living two completely different lives because there is no one you have invited into your life to walk with you and help assure your success in this journey. Without an accountability partner, you are an easy target for the enemy to hit because there is no one in your world to warn you. Entering into a relationship with an accountability partner is not for those who want a shaky relationship with Christ. It will not benefit those who want to live like the devil Monday through Saturday, but have the power of God come Sunday. It is for those who are not satisfied with second best in their spiritual walk and would rather upgrade continuously as their walk progresses. No real man of God prays for a mediocre woman. He prefers to have God's divine best for his life. I dare you to upgrade your life. Make yourself accountable to someone. Do it today and watch God change your life.

SLB's Testimony

The thing that most engages and most impresses me about you and your teaching style is that you say specifically what you mean. You get right to the point and don't mince words. You also don't say things harshly or in a way that would put someone in condemnation for having done wrong. You simply and calmly say, "As women of God we are to do this because...," or " As women of God we don't engage in that because ..." Sometimes it makes so much "spiritual" common sense that it makes my practical common sense look stupid! And this way of teaching helps me to have a paradigm shift in the way that I have thought about things like men and dating. It is not intimidating; it is real life and it is supported with all the love you have, which is a lot. You care and it shows. I love the way you put it out there but balance it with the word of God and with the fact that you say, "For me this is why I choose or we choose to do this." I can receive that. I imagine others easily receive it too.

I also greatly enjoyed the "Get Yourself Together" nuggets. Those were really good to know. I especially found a lot of value in the skits, the real life examples you presented to us. The skits were like "simulation" of real life experiences and I thought I knew what I'd do in certain situations, but in acting it out, I got stuck and was speechless sometimes. But they were fun and eye opening and showed me how a woman of God is supposed to respond in situations.

Fay, you present yourself in such a quiet and unassuming manner that who would know such wisdom and love was housed in such a small frame? That is how I know with clarity the power of God is working in you. I know you love me by the amount of time you spent talking with me about things that concerned me. I know you love your children by raising them in the admonition of God's word. And I know you love your husband by respecting him as the headship and spiritual leader over your house. So in short, I see how you use God's kingdom principles in your life in a very practical way and that is a powerful witness to me.

Now that I have this information, I desire to walk in God's principles of courtship and marriage relationship. I am approached by non-Christian men or carnal Christian men who still have ideas of dating and the like. It is very frustrating. Where are the men who desire God's heart like I do? Where are the Christian men who want a true Christian woman? But at the same time, I am encouraged because I'm better able to "see" and identify this man of God for me. My sense of "sight" is a lot keener and there is great comfort and rest in that. I imagine this is the "rest" God calls us to be in as we trust and wait on him for the desires of our hearts.

Love you Fay

Get Yourself Together!: Cleanliness Is Next To Godliness: Part III

Let's go back to that bathroom we talked about earlier. Ladies, girls, are you really ready to get yourself together? You have to because these are issues we cannot allow ourselves to take into our marriages.

Lord give me a man!

You may be thinking that these are areas that are not important. When you marry, it's not just you anymore. How crushed would your little heart be if your husband, after having observed your cleaning habits, commented, "When I married you, I thought you were clean. Girl, you are some kind of nasty." Girls, envision your bathroom in your mind. Got it? Okay, now, see that small trash can beside the toilet, the one over running with used sanitary napkins? The same trash can visitors see when their feet are swinging over your toilet seat. Yes, *that* trash can. Okay, well, tell me something: What's wrong with putting objects of such a nature in a small plastic bag and disposing of it immediately outside? You may think that it shouldn't matter what's in your trash can because you do not allow anyone to use your personal or master bathroom. Yes, it does matter because those things stink and need to be disposed of quickly, and not at the end of the week when you clean your bathroom. Whatever cleaning habits you have now will be the same cleaning habits you have when you marry. It may be your bathroom now but when God sends the man of God, who best suits you into your life as husband, if your smelly stuff is in the trash can now, that's where it will be when it's his bathroom, too. The poor guy will have to endure it because he won't want to hurt your feelings. Let's make a change now. Don't fight it. Allow God to change you from the inside out and upgrade you in those personal areas. Here's an idea: Get a trash can that has a lid of some sort. The best kinds are the cans whose lids swing back and forth. You can deposit your "unmentionables" into

Accountability

the can and no one will be the wiser. If you keep air fresher at the bottom of the can under the can liner, no one will smell the wiser, either. It's a good practice to have, especially in your guest bathroom. Guests may also make deposits and if you don't check often, you can end up with a smelly bathroom after a day or two. So, let's review: Trash can with the lid that swings back and forth; deodorizer (the one I like the best is the kind that usually hangs in the toilet because they deodorize and lasts longer but aren't overbearing); and liner or trash bag. So, if you walk by your bathroom trash can and you see pastel colors hanging over the rim of your trash can or detect a pungent odor, girl it is time to **Get Yourself Together!**

Affirmation: I don't know if cleanliness is next to godliness, but I do know that the trash can is next to me when I'm on the toilet and I won't let it stink!

-6-
Single Parenting in Christ Is A Lie

For many reasons, Christian women find themselves raising their children without the father in the home. In many cases, these women are unhappy and bitter about their status. Whether they want to admit it or not, bitterness lies within their hearts because things did not work out as planned.

Parenting is not the easiest calling, but we are called to do it. The children under your care have a destiny given to them by God, a reason for which they were born. It is our job as mothers to nurture them and pour into them what we can. We need to center them around believers who can pour into them as well. Just like adults, children need confirmation of who they are in God. They may not always listen to what their parents tell them. If they hear it from someone else, they might get it.

Pour It On

Since you can't do it all by yourself, pray and ask God to send you someone you can trust to pour into the lives of your children in a loving caring way. Be open and watch for those believers who really take to your child and seek God as to the purpose of that person being in your child's life. You may want to approach that person after you have prayed and ask them to consider becoming your child's Godmother or big brother or sister who will add godly direction and counsel in their lives. Children do not care how much you know until they know how much you care. When they know you care, you will then have their ear.

Each one of my children has at least one adult in their lives with whom they have relationship. Those relationships are growing because they are being cultivated. Pray that your child would find favor in someone's sight that would desire to spend time with him or her. I have found in my experiences and the experiences of others, that it truly does take a village to raise a child.

You Can't Be the Daddy

I often hear single mothers who are raising their children without a father in the home say, "I have to be the mom and the dad." While I sympathize with your situation, I have a startling realization for you.

You can't father your child! Woman of God, you have been called to be a mother and if you can seek God on how to perfect some of those areas that you may be weak in as a mother, your child will be the better for it. Don't spend time driving in the wrong lane. Stay in your lane. You have spent so much time trying to be mom and dad and the truth is you are not anointed to father. You have more than enough to do as a mother. There is so much required of you by God as a mother. If you can allow yourself to be set free from the idea that have to make up for the fact that dad's not in the home or in your child's life, you will begin to see a change in your life and the life of your child. Just be who you are. You are mom, not the daddy!

Let the Father, father

There are cases when the father wants nothing to do with the child and other cases where the father can't be a part of the child's life due to incarceration or even death. There are men who want to have a hand in raising their children but are not living under the same roof as the child. It is possible for a father to be a father and reside in another home. We women fail to recognize the damage that is done in the lives of our children when they have a father who wants to spend time with them but we do all we can to prevent it. Let the father be a father. There are so many things our children miss out on when we deprive them of their fathers because of our selfish reasons. There are certain circumstances where, due to the safety of the child or even yourself, you feel you must keep the children away from the father. If that is not the case and the father wants to be involved, please allow him. That father may not have all you want him to have or be all you want him to be. To make or pass judgment on him would conflict with the word of God. Consider yourself and your walk with God. Have you arrived? The last time you looked up the word "perfect" did you see your picture? Of course not. We all have our crosses to bear, so extend mercy. You would ask the same if the tables were turned. Stop trying to control the man.

Ladies you know how to work it. If he doesn't do what you want him to do or what you think he should do, you not only talk about him, often in front of the children, but you also deny him the chance to spend time with his children. Why do some mothers play such cruel games? Let the Father be a father if he is willing. Your child needs whatever God would have him to receive from the time spent with his or her father. If a father is only good to you when his money is good, you are using him and you are teaching your children to use him. This is especially dangerous if you have a daughter who witnesses such behavior. If you are not careful, she will grow up to be just like you and use men, too.

Watch Your Confession

It never fails. Every time I ask a woman with children if she is a single parent, she will reply "yes". It doesn't matter is she has been divorced, widowed or never married. Her answer is still the same. Yes.

Single parenting means to parent alone. If both parents live separately, but parent together, they are not considered "single parents". It may not be the way you envisioned it, but it is the truth. If the father is doing something in the area of parenting, give him credit for it and perhaps he will do more.

"But I am doing it on my own, the dad's not even in the picture. I don't even get child support; it's just my children and me." You still are not a single parent! Now before you shut this book and send me hate email, allow me to explain.

Ephesians 3:20 says that, "God is able to do exceedingly abundantly more than we can ask or imagine, according to His power that is at work within us." He is our teacher, our comforter and our Father. Mom, you are not doing it alone. Don't give yourself that much credit. Some credit, yes, but not all. The plain fact is that God is helping you to parent your child and when you declare yourself to be a single parent you are actually subtracting God from the equation. God gets no glory when you call yourself a single parent. You have no idea all that God does for you on a daily basis to assist you in parenting. The truth of the matter is that if God were to remove the hand of favor from your life, you would then know what it felt like to be a single parent. You would be totally alone and on your own.

We are so use to God's hand that we take it for granted. Whether you know it or not, there is grace from God that sits upon your life to do what it is that you need to do as a parent. Don't take it for granted. So, the next time you are asked about your status as a mother, don't be so quick to take all the credit. If the child's father is doing anything for the child, show some humility and mention him. When your parenting is complimented say," Thank you. I'll share that with his or her father." Sharing the credit is humbling and will aid in the softening of your heart.

This is still all a part of preparing for marriage. If these issues are not dealt with before marrying, they could put a great strain on your relationship. A man of God may pray for a woman with children but certainly not for a woman with children who has unresolved issues with the father. With the help of God, clean up this area before you marry.

Get the Little Buggers in Line

During the 80s there was an animated program on TV featuring children who were unpredictable in their behavior. The program was very popular at the time. The characters were comical. One character had insects constantly flying around him because his diaper was smelly while another may have picked his nose. All the children were bad! If any of you reading right now are over the age of 30, you know what show I am talking about. You get the point. If these children were up for adoption, they would remain there.

My question to you is, "How closely do your children resemble the characters of that 80s show?" Think about it. If you were honest with yourself, could you admit that family and friends have made comments about the poor behavior of your children? Do people encourage you to visit without your kids? Do all of your family members get quiet when you mention you need a baby sitter? If you can answer yes to any of these questions, you have your work cut out for you or you should hope that the program that I spoke of makes a comeback so your children can audition.

Women of God, it makes no sense what good men have to put up with from your children just to get to know you. A woman once told me a story about a guy who was interested in her. Every time they got together in an attempt to get to know one another, her son would constantly interrupt. Whenever the man spent time with them, the son would be jumping on the furniture and was just flat out rude. He also lacked table manners. This bothered the gentleman. The mother constantly made excuses for the child's behavior but the man knew that the child behaved this way every day. The mother had placed few restrictions on her son which made shopping trips a total nightmare. When the gentleman made an attempt to discuss his concerns with the mother, she became offended and defensive telling him, with her neck and eyes rolling, that their home was her son's home. He should be comfortable doing whatever he wanted to do in his own home. She continued to rant, stating that the gentleman was a guest in her home and that guests do eventually leave. Her son could stay for as long as he wanted and do what he wanted. If the son wanted to write on the leather furniture, she could get it cleaned. If he wrote on the wall she would just paint it. She defended her son by saying a home is to be enjoyed by the children and not by just adults only. If the son wanted to join in on their conversations, she was fine with that. "I keep no secrets from my son," she added, "and if you don't like the fact that he is six years old and still sleeps with me, it's because he doesn't like sleeping by himself. I told him he could sleep with me as long as he wanted. Whoever God has for me will have to understand."

Whew! That was a mouthful, wasn't it? The mother was so busy defending the inappropriate behavior of her son, she could have very well been missing out on the *one* God had intended for her. Another good man gone, but, she still has her son!

What are the chances of this woman ever being close or ready for marriage? Do you find yourself relating to this story? Are you anywhere in this scenario?

I can remember when my husband and I knew that we were going to marry. He allowed me to meet his daughter. While I was getting to know her, I observed that she was always very well behaved and well mannered. I thought the little girl was putting on airs. If I gave it enough time, she would begin to show her true colors. Boy, was I wrong. She really was a sweet little six year old girl. If we were out shopping and she was told she could not have an item that she wanted, she did not pout or throw temper tantrums. She would simply reply, "Okay, daddy." The behavior of this sweet little girl was a direct result of both parents parenting. Although her father did not live with her or her mother, he was still a very active part of her life. Guess what? Both parents gave one another credit for their role in parenting. They were civil with one another which made me feel comfortable going into a marital relationship with him. What I witnessed was two parents raising one child. The parents didn't reside under the same roof, but they touched base with one another. They kept a level of respect for each other which made it easier on the child. The fact that she was a well behaved child spoke to the consistency in parenting from both her mom and dad. So Alexis, if you're reading this, don't let your head swell. Rhonda Brown, thanks for all you have invested in that cute little six year old. It made things so much easier transitioning from single life with no kids to a married life with one. This chapter is dedicated to both of you. May God richly prosper you.

-7-
Redeeming The Time II: Self-Development

Get Outta Town!

Single women, this is your time to venture out and see the world —- or at least a piece of it. You will bring some experiences into your marriage. When your husband asks where you have been all his life, you shouldn't say, "Right here." You should be able to share with him the places you've been and some of the experiences you've had. You could share that you saw an armadillo when you traveled to Texas with your best friend. You can share the experiences you had when you went to a conference in California. You can talk about how much you enjoyed seeing palm trees for the first time in Florida; or how fresh lobsters tasted in Maine.

Traveling assists in your being well-rounded, creates a host of experiences, and affords you the opportunity to gain some firsthand knowledge of the areas you visited. If you want to see Europe, do your homework to find out what all is involved in traveling to that part of the world. Call a travel agent for information, determine the cost, and set up a plan to go. There are also ads in the paper that list cheap vacations. You can also join ministry tours to other countries. Consider ministries you enjoy watching on TV and contact them for information on upcoming tours they may be taking. Go online and do a search on ministry tours. Staying in the town you were born for the rest of your life without branching out every once in a while can cause you to see the world one sided. Broaden your horizons. Get out and experience the world with or without friends.

Affirmation: Airports are full of planes. I just have to pick a destination and purchase my ticket. I think I will.

Finances

Now is the time to get your money in check. Start by creating a budget. If your household consists of one or several people, you still need a budget. A budget will help you to know how much money you have to work with and where it's going when you do work with it.

Many single people like yourself get paid, Hopefully pay bills, and then spend what's left as they see fit. One problem with this train of thought is that before the week is over, the money is gone. Then you can't give an account to where it has gone. It is time for us to grow up in this respect. No man of God prays for a wife whose money is a mess.

The first thing believers are required to do is tithe. Many believers feel that if they tithe, they will experience great blessings. The blessing on our finances is two-part. One part is giving God his ten percent tithe and the other part is what we do with the remaining ninety percent.

Affirmation: I know I received a pay check less than two weeks ago. I don't know where all my money went but enough is enough. It's time to make a change!

Health

Single ladies, tell me something. Who wants a wife who doesn't care about the quality of her health? There are things that we can do on a daily basis to care for ourselves in order to help maintain a better quality of life. We can refrain from smoking. There are books that can aid in eating healthier meals versus dieting. Dieting may bring about temporary change but it is something that must be continued to maintain what it yields. However, changing eating habits and eating healthier is a lifestyle that will yield even better results.

We can do many things to change some of our negative eating habits. Instead of wasting money on foods high in salt content and saturated fats such as fast food chains and microwavable meals, we should buy healthy foods from the grocery store and cook ourselves a good meal. It may take a little more of your time, but your body will be the better for it. We live in such a fast-paced society, always on the go, that our bodies are not given the opportunity to properly digest a meal. Sitting down to eat your meal will allow the body to break down the food to distribute the nutrients and get rid of the rest. That's the natural side of things. The spiritual side is that our bodies are the temples of the Holy Spirit. I admit I have seen some pretty sad looking temples. If God were to bring judgment on us for how we have cared for our temples, would you be in trouble. Most of the illnesses we experience are directly related to how poorly we have cared for ourselves. We can spiritualize it if we want by blaming the devil when we get sick. However, this won't change the pattern in our lives of constantly getting sick, getting better, and getting sick again. If you know your lifestyle requires you to run your body non-stop, change your lifestyle.

If you're the type of person who cannot live without fried chicken, try oven fried. It's healthier and tastes just as good without all the added fat from the cooking oil. Who wants to receive a bride with unhealthy eating habits? Prior to coming to the marriage table, we should do what we can to correct health issues that exist and choose a healthier way of caring for our temple. If God can't trust us to take care of our own bodies, how will He be able to trust us to take care of a spouse? You know what you need to do. You need to "get yourself together!

Also, do your breast exams and get your annual physical. If there is a particular illness common in your family, find out what you can do to cut down the risk of developing it. Schedule and keep your appointment with your OB/GYN. You may not want to go, but let's grow up and open up!

Affirmation: If the food I am putting in my body isn't coming out of my body on a daily basis, then I had better find out why it's still in me and how long it plans to stay. This is just not healthy.

Kick It Up A Notch

A single woman can do so much to work on the outside of her temple. A woman once shared a story with me about an acquaintance who commented that two of them were going to have to doctor themselves up with more makeup, hair done, etc. in order for them to get a husband, or at least a man, who still found them attractive. "We are too plain," the acquaintance said to her. The woman asked my opinion on the matter. There were several things that I told her and I will share one of them with you. If you have to wear more make up and get your hair done once a week instead of bi-weekly, then that is what he will be attracted to. What happens when you wash your face after taking off of your hair piece? What you do to get him is what you have to do to keep him. Never change who you are to get a man.

Upgrading is always good, but only in the areas where you need it. If you have a four year degree in your field, then perhaps you may want to get your master's. Always consider classes and training sessions on your job that you can sign up for. Always find yourself learning more in your field to keep from becoming stagnated. When it comes time to downsize on your job, who do you think they will get rid of? The one who is working on himself to be the best employee he can be through training sessions that aren't mandatory or the one who just gives the required eight hour shift and goes home? Who would you keep and who would you let go?

Let's discuss your wardrobe. If your vintage looks like you purchased them in the clothes section of an antique shop, you may need to believe God for a new wardrobe. Find a woman at church or a good friend whose wardrobe you like and ask them to go shopping with you. Let them know that you would like their advice on how you select clothing that looks and feels good on you. You're not trying to change your image. You just want to enhance it to reflect the changes taking place on the inside of you.

What about makeup? Honey, red lipstick is just not your color, neither is that color eye shadow you've been wearing. You may say, "But Fay, how am I supposed to know what looks good on me and what doesn't?" When you look at a clown and you see a resemblance, then you don't know what you're doing. Don't feel bad. Ever hear of Mary K? Their representatives are trained in makeup application and more. Seek out one and ask for a makeover. If you like the outcome, purchase the items she used on you and practice until you get it right. I am not big on makeup; however, for my wedding, I wanted someone who knew what they were doing to handle it. I didn't want the song, "Send in the clown," to play as I came down the aisle. I called my cousin from New York to help. I can't tell you how many compliments I got that day. When people see my wedding pictures now, one of the first things they notice is the quality of the makeup. My gown was made by one of Maryland's finest dressmakers, and my hair… let's not talk about my hair. Not a strand of hair was out of place. I paid top dollar for it. The level of excellence was of the highest. Why did I invest in myself that way? Because I'm worth it and so are you. Investing in yourself not only counts on your wedding day but for your way of life. This demonstrates the quality of woman that you are.

Pray and ask God to show you where you need to change for the better, and then begin to move forward. What do you think your husband will say if asked to describe his very first impression of you? What words will he use to describe your appearance? Got you thinking, don't I? Then, girl, *"get yourself together!"*

Affirmation: I have taken time to assess the quality of woman I am and I determined that I am of the highest quality. But, I must still demand better of myself. Mediocre won't do. It is a known fact that a wife is a reflection of her husband and if she is poorly dressed and hair in despair, he looks bad. So, I'm working on myself now before he comes into my life.

Get Yourself Together: Giving

It is biblical to give. We often want others to give when we have a need or a want, but how often do you open your wallet or give of your time, resources, or personal possessions? You may not have much, but if you keep your fist closed tight in order not to lose what you have, nothing can get in. Don't be tight. Ask God to give you a giving heart so that you may help a brother or sister you see has a need. We, as believers, like to say, "Pressed down, shaken together and running over shall men give unto you." (Luke 6:38) Often, we fail to quote the first part which states, "Give and it shall be given to you." Tell me, on the way to church, do you stop by the store to get change for five dollars so you can have a few singles for the offering? If you pastor a church, how financially fruitful would the church be with a congregation of givers just like you in it? When you're out with your girlfriends, do you rise to be a blessing? Within the next thirty days, why don't you call three friends and treat them out to dinner? Show them that you appreciate them. Once a month or every three months, take an extra fifty dollars and give it in the offering at church. Maybe also give anonymously to a particular ministry that may have been overlooked. Perhaps you can offer to ministries like the nursery or prison ministry. Ask God to put someone in your path who could use a financial blessing. The next time you see them, place twenty dollars in their hand and tell them, "God wants you to know that He is thinking about you." God has not given you what you have for you to keep it all for yourself. God blesses us so that we can be a blessing to the kingdom of God. Everything we need is in the kingdom; and we make up the kingdom of God. If you desire a Godly marriage, you cannot have an attitude that is all about you. Consider others. In marriage, giving is a requirement. If you can't give to your fellow brother, how will you be able to give to your husband? When you cannot give, you are not ready for a fruitful marriage. When all you do is give to yourself and the bill collectors, begin to ask God to teach you how to become a better steward with your finances and how to work the giving principle of Luke 6:38 and *"get yourself together!"*

Affirmation: The money I am blessed with can only be a blessing to others if I release it.

-8-
Food For Thought

No Hook Ups

I have heard it said it is not what you know, but who you know when it comes to getting something done. This saying has to be one of the most truthful statements used by Christians and non-Christians alike. It basically means that when you desire to have something, and you know how to go about getting it without going through any hassle, you'll do it. You may know someone who knows someone who can get the job done or provide the service to fulfill the need. That person has "hooked you up". Well, I know of another type of hook-up that went terribly wrong:

A woman, who had been through several non-productive relationships in her life, was set up with a man her sister had met and gotten to know fairly well. She told the man about her sister, including the fact that her sister had several children. The man became interested and wanted to meet her. The sister "hooked them up." Eventually, the man moved into the home with the woman and her children. It wasn't long before the man starting building the woman's confidence up in him by paying all her bills and being the man he knew she wanted. It wasn't long before the woman became dependent upon him and the two ended up getting married. Think the story ends happily? Not at all. The man began making sexual threats and passes at the woman's daughter which resulted in the daughter leaving home. After years of abuse, the marriage ended in divorce. It was later believed that the daughter had lied on this hardworking superman who rescued the single mother from financial hardship. That "hook up" cost the family more than can ever be told. The intentions of the sister were good; the hook-up was not a good idea. You do not know a person as well as God does. What may seem good on the outside could be spoiled on the inside. Let God do the work. Scripture says that, "there is a way that seems right to a man, but in the end it leads to death." (Proverbs 14:12)

You are probably thinking of couples you know who are happy and were brought together either by you or by someone else. I will not deny that there are times when we are right on when we think of two people and how compatible we feel they are. What if there was also just that one time when we are wrong and as a result of the "hook up," one person drags the other through hell. How would we feel? We would probably vow to never again play matchmaker. Although the decision seemed like a sound one, what was the cost and who paid it to cause us well-intentioned match makers to get it? We all make mistakes. Yet, it only takes one extreme mistake to cost someone their daughter, family or life.

When I was single, there were a few girls I roomed with. They all knew Levelle and one of them even grew up with him. They had talked and all believed that they knew who the perfect man would be for me: Levelle. They never shared his name with me, but I knew they had talked and agreed that Levelle would be the perfect one for me. Not once did they ever try to hook me up. They sat back and watched God do the work. If you have a friend who you feel is compatible with another person, instead of stepping ahead of God by trying to fix them up, consider, why not consider praying a simple prayer like, "Lord, I bring before you (couple's name). They seem perfect for each other. Since you are a God who knows all things, I will yield to you, Lord. If their coming together will honor you, work in their hearts the preparation for marriage. In your name, I pray, Amen."

Do Not Be Afraid To Fight!

When Adam had sinned against God, he hid himself. The word tells us that Adam hid himself because he was afraid. This instance marks the introduction of the Spirit of Fear onto the earth. David, on the other hand, was not fearful when he ran up to meet Goliath. David knew who he was or at least Whose he was. David not only identified who his enemy was by calling him an uncircumcised Philistine, but he told Goliath that he came in the name of the Lord. Like it or not, we believers must fight from time to time. There is always a battle going on in some fashion during our Christian walk. I want you to always remember that every time a war is waged on your life, you wrestle not against flesh and blood but against principalities, against powers, against rulers of the darkness of this world (Ephesians:6:12).

The mere fact that you are born again is a threat to the kingdom of darkness. Satan is aware of the potential dangers involved of two believers coveting together in marriage. The damage to his kingdom stands to be a lot worse when two come together as one in covenant. You may have to fight in order to receive what God has for you. There will be traps you will encounter and counterfeits, disguised as originals, you will face. The enemy does not want you to succeed nor to achieve that which God has in store for you. He can delay you from being prepared or try to keep you from being focused. He will do it. If he can keep you from being faithful, he will do it. Keep in mind that one of the tricks of the enemy is to get us to fight physically that which is spiritual. Trying to fight a spiritual battle with physical weapons is a pure waste of time, and not to mention, harmful to believers. When the dust clears, we leave another battle defeated. Now is the time to learn about warfare. As you upgrade from one level to another, you will encounter a new level of devils. It is to your benefit to learn how to defeat these devils before they launch an attack on you. While you are working your way through these upcoming months, spend more time in prayer learning all you can about spiritual warfare. In doing so, you will learn to stop fighting a spiritual war carnally (I Corinthians 10:3-4).

I also strongly encourage you to read the following book: *Teach My Hands To War* by Kemi Searcy (New Voice Publishing, 2005) Now is the time to read it and not when you are in the heat of battle. Do not allow yourself to be caught in battle, holding your sword, asking, "How does this thing work, again?" You have weapons that are unbeatable. You just have to learn how to use them. The good news to all this is that you do not have to fight alone. You have your Lord and Savior, as well as other believers who are in your life, to walk with you. The same will also fight alongside you.

Time Lost

I knew that by the grace of God, I would one day become a wife and a mother. I also knew that the place I was currently in left no room for my getting caught up in fantasy land. Fantasy land is where we single women visit our wedding day in our minds. We fantasize about the songs that will be sung, the groom standing at the altar, the wedding gown we will wear, the reception afterwards, and so on. I needed some work to be done on the inside of me. I did not have time to waste on vain imaginations. Unlike most women, the little time I did spend imagining, I spent on what it would be like to be married. I imagined more on the marriage itself than of the ceremony leading up to it. We spend too much time focusing on things of the future instead of what is in the here and now. We give too much of our attention to things out of season. This is the trick of the enemy. He desires to take our focus off of the purpose of God for our lives today and push it far into the future. The future is only part of what we should think about. Our present is what we have to live out in order to sail into what is promised to us.

When I told God that I wanted the companionship of marriage, He told me to only be faithful and focus. I did just that. Concentrating on doing this prevented my mind from wondering too far into the future. I was about the here and now. I focused on what God was trying to work out of me and what He wanted to work within me, and what He wanted to work through me. I was being faithful and focused. After a while, I could see the changes in my life and so could others. I could see the benefits of laying aside, not necessarily the sin, but the weight that would easily beset me. Truly, that time allowed me to run with patience the race that was set before me. God began shaving off things in my life that did not need to be there. From time to time, He would pour in things that there was no room for. He was preparing me for marriage. Time was short. I had no idea what little time was left to allow God to remake me before my Mighty Man of God would arrive. From the time that I confessed my heart to God about wanting companionship to the day that Levelle approached me about marriage was six months and two weeks. God enrolled me into His "six-month marriage preparation class" two weeks after I asked for a companion.

Redeem The Time (Ephesians 5:15)

Redeeming the time it is about what you do while you wait. Are you productive in the wait? Redeeming the time is maximizing your wait. You want to accomplish what you can, while you can. If you got married today, what areas of your life would you wish you had worked on prior to it? Perhaps it would not be such a bad idea to stop reading now, and make a list of those areas you know you need to work on until you have mastered them. We tend to live our lives like we take antibiotics. The directions say take until bottle is empty, meaning, do not just take a few doses until you feel better and discard the rest. Finish the medication. Instead, we look for an indicator of change and then we do nothing more in that area because change is visible. That is where we go wrong. If you only take the antibiotic until you feel better, the symptoms usually return within a few days. You celebrated prematurely and now you are more ill than you were when you first started taking the medication. The instructions clearly told you to finish the bottle. Obedience is better than sacrifice.

In our lives, we need not to just do better in the areas that need work; we need to concentrate on mastering those areas that need work. To master something does not necessarily mean being the best at whatever it is you are trying to master. Mastering something means to do your very best in accordance to the purpose of God in your life. When I decided that I was ready for marriage, I had reached the point where I maximized my singleness. I had mastered certain areas of my life as a single woman of God not desiring marriage and was ready for the next level. I had a lot of work still to do and much to master, but I had mastered several areas in my life prior to my desiring to be married. I wanted to redeem the time of my waiting and I often found that I was giving it my best.

Too Late To Turn Back Now

Most women want to be married. There is no shame in saying it, but very few of us think we need real preparation for marriage. All the preparation most women get is from friends, sixty minute talk shows, or advice they pick up along their life's long journey from bitter women who have suffered heartbreaks. It is futile to seek advice from a heart who only knows bitterness. The Bible says that out of the fullness of the heart the mouth speaks (Matthew 12:34). The words of a bitter woman can only mean death to a relationship. Learn to keep your business between you and God.

The divorce rate among Christians is said to be higher than the rate of those who are still single. We must begin to do something different if we expect to see a change for the better. If we want to be successful, we must first prepare. It is foolish to attempt to achieve or conquer anything without first preparing. One cannot expect to go into battle and win if he has not first prepared for the battle. In order to elevate to the next level and be successful on that level, God must first prepare you for it. It is time to grow up and allow God to work in our lives without giving Him a fight. There are many things we all must continue to work on, especially before the arrival of the man of God. We must also work on these things daily.

I trust that you will move quickly towards change in order to not only be easily identified as the woman of his dreams but to also fortify the walls of your mind for the storms in marriage that are sure to come. Don't put this book down, having been offended, but rather encouraged to change to the next level which may include marriage.

I hope that you have been journaling daily in your Lord, Give Me a Man Companion Journal. The purpose is to help you develop a habit of reading the word, praying, and keeping track in your journal what God shares with you daily. Take time to read every day and then spend some time in prayer listening for what your Commander and Chief has to say. Please don't cheat yourself by not doing this. At the end of the six months, you should have a book full of thoughts, responses and visible growth. Aren't you tired of seeing no growth in your life? Then read, pray and journal daily. Learn, as a single woman, to meet the Lord daily. If you do this faithfully for twenty-one days, you will form a habit of it. It will change your life.

When you are done with this journal, don't throw it away. Hold on to it. Reread it later to see how you've grown and to remind you of the things God has told you while you were in prayer with Him. What you hear from Him will change who you are as a woman. Take this time seriously. You are preparing for success. Imagine how blessed the man of God and your future marriage will be when he finds out that you have worked on yourself in preparation for him. "Be strong in the Lord and in His mighty power put on the whole armor of God that you may be able to stand in the evil day." (Ephesians 6: 10-11)

Cold Is Just Cold

Which is colder? A cold shower or a cold bath? It has been said that when a single person experiences sexual urges, all he or she needs to do is take a cold shower and Bam! the urge is gone. There are others who don't have a shower, so taking a cold bath is the next best thing. It may have meant only partial submersion but it did the trick. Some of you are saying, "TMI (Too much Information)". Those who want to be real are saying, "What's a girl to do?"

While I know that single Christians have no business engaging in sexually gratifying acts of any kind, I do acknowledge that urges are real. The question is not, what do I do if I do not have a shower. Rather, what can I do to prevent the urges from surfacing?

There are many things we can do in order to be proactive. This is a flesh issue and must be dealt with quickly. Bringing our bodies under subjection to the authority of the Holy Spirit is a start. Speaking to our flesh and commanding it to obey what the word says is another way of bringing our bodies under subjection. We must crucify our flesh. The Apostle Paul said, "I die daily", and so must we.

I have learned over the years that some believers spend more time with self-help books in an attempt to get a quick cure. Others spend time in the presence of God getting direction or a word from the Lord on how to overcome a hurdle in their lives. While I do not discourage reading self-help books, I do discourage doing so in the place of getting your answer from God.

Relying on books more than God can easily eliminate our opportunity for relationship and spiritual growth. When we spend time with God, we get to know our God as the answer for everything, plain and simple. Don't get me wrong. There is nothing wrong with purchasing a book that speaks to your situation. I am asking that you allow that book to serve as confirmation of the word God gave you, or longs to give you in prayer. Go to Him first and on to the book store second. I believe there comes a time when we need to go to God for ourselves and share our heart with him in order to allow him to speak to our situations personally. Again, I encourage you to take time in prayer with your situation. In the process, get to know God in a newer way. After you have spent time in the presence of God about bringing your body under subjection, He may lead you to contact me. Do so and I will personally pray for you in this area.

-9-
From His Point Of View

I Know She Is Not The One

Often, there are more things that a man of God does not want in a wife versus what he does. For some reason, his "What I Don't Want In A Wife" list is always longer.

This part of the book is not written to make you feel as if are you are not wanted. It is written to cause you to take a closer look at yourself to see if there is anything on that list that you can relate to. If so, you may want to bring them before the Lord and ask Him to do an about a change in your heart that will affect a change in your life. A meek and quiet spirit should be our goal to attain and maintain. Do everything without grumbling and complaining or arguing so that you may become blameless as pure children of God, without fault, in a crooked and depraved generation. One of my oldest and wisest spiritual mentors, Ms.

Carrie Jackson, gave me the best piece of marital advice. She said that wives would fare much better in their marriages if they would learn when to keep their mouths shut.

Philippians 2:3-8 states:

> Do nothing out of selfish ambition or vain conceit. Rather, in humility value others above yourselves, not looking to your own interests but each of you to the interests of the others. In your relationships with one another, have the same mindset as Christ Jesus: Who, being in very nature [God, did not consider equality with God something to be used to his own advantage; rather, he made himself nothing by taking the very nature of a servant, being made in human likeness. And being found in appearance as a man, he humbled himself by becoming obedient to death- even death on a cross!

Some of the key words or attributes in this scripture are humility, servant, and obedient.

Throughout the course of writing this book, I asked single men to share with me things that told them that a woman was not for them. I also asked married men to consider the same question. Several men said the same things and here are a few responses:

- A smoking Christian
- A woman who lacks self- confidence and is not submitted to God
- A controlling woman

- A woman who smokes and or drinks; also, a head strong woman; woman who does not care for herself. It would scare me to think that my daughter may look up to someone like that as an example
- A sloppy or messy woman: one who has a bad relationship with her father; it may speak to how she will relate to me as a husband
- A non-compatible lifestyle
- Controlling
- Insecure
- Argumentative
- Promiscuous
- Not being able to resolve conflict in an honest, intimate way
- I want a young lady who has kept herself and one who is pure in heart, dedicated to God and virtuous
- One who has her own personal relationship with the Lord and gets most of her fulfillment from Christ. I cannot be her "be all and end all." I should be able to tell her how I feel without a blowout. She must be able to resolve conflict in a healthy manner.

I also asked men of God how they felt when a woman would approach them with the following statement: God told me you are my husband. Here is what one person said:

"I have heard that God is more than willing and able to speak to both parties, not just one person. The woman was brought to the man. If she hears, then she should wait. If he hears, he should encourage her to hear from God. Fast, pray, and get a clear word from God. Remember Noah? Although he was on dry land, he did not exit the ark, but waited to hear from God. This thing is serious!"

Ladies, I ask you to consider what you just read and be honest with yourself and point out the things that God still needs to work out of you.

Levelle's Testimony: From the Wolf to the Sheep

I wanted to share my testimony with women to give them insight into the mind of a predator. I feel led to talk about something I haven't talked about in over fifteen years. And when I did speak about it, it was solely for the purpose of deliverance from my past sins.

I want to say that I am qualified to speak on this subject. I am not coming from a behavioral therapist standpoint, but from the standpoint of my own life experiences.

Between the ages of 16 and 21, I was hurt by two different girlfriends whose actions significantly altered the course of my life and fashioned how I would begin to treat women. I won't bore you with the gory details for it is not what is important. What is important, however, is that I show you how the mind of a predator works, so that you can be on the lookout from this day forward.

When I was growing up, a "player" gave me a piece of sordid advice. He said, "You don't want to spend time chasing the woman you want. Spend time chasing the woman who wants you." He was so right. I started out dating, wining and dining women, only to get a kiss at the end of the day. In some cases, it took six months to a year to get what I was after. I didn't mind because I was perfecting my skills during those early days of stalking. You see, I had to be a chameleon because the woman I was interested in would not be interested in me; not the real me. I had to become the man I thought she wanted. I would talk on the phone for hours and hours getting to know her. I would ask questions to get her to talk about herself. Did you know people like to talk about themselves more than anything else? It's true. So, I would open the car door if she liked that kind of thing. If she liked bad boys, I would pick her up in my truck and we would do what I thought bad boys do.

If she was trying to be a good girl, I would ask her if I could go to church with her. Sometimes I would get a lot of points just for asking. I remember once that this girl told me that no matter what, she's never intimate within the first six month period of the dating period. I made a mental note but replied, "Really?" Well, she meant what she said. Six months later we had sex. We had sex once, and then I broke up with her after that. Lord, please don't allow me to face the penalty of my sins.

"But God demonstrates his own love for us in this: While we were yet sinners, Christ died for us." (Romans 5:8)

I said all that to say this: The man that pursues you may not be the man for you. He may be a counterfeit looking for whomever he may devour. Seek the Lord.

Hear from the Lord and know that you know he is the one before you entertain him.

Remember the advice the "player" gave me? Remember, he said not to pursue the woman I was interested in but to pursue the woman who was interested in me. The stories I accounted earlier were of women who were interested in me. Women who spoke into their own hearts, "I would like to get to know you better." Please note that a wolf can smell and sense when a woman is interested in him. I dated so many women because they liked the way I treated women. I have had sex with friends of friends, sisters and best friends. Only because I could see that they enjoyed how I was treating the woman I was with. These women never admitted the reasons for wanting to be with me; I just sensed it. I really don't know how to describe it but it's like I paid attention to women and could tell what their insecurities were by the way they carried themselves. Whatever area she was insecure in, I made it a point to compliment and make her feel better. My games ranged from paying attention to her children to helping her feel confident about her cooking abilities. Whatever area she felt weak in, I was there to help build her up. The wolf always scans the herd for the weak ones, and then he attacks!

I have had relationships with a lot of women that most men were intimidated by. I dated the daughter of a professional heavy weight boxing champion; I dated wealthy women and even a Jennifer Lopez look-alike; and all these women had one thing in common: Low self-esteem. There was an area within

Summary

So, before you fall backwards onto your bed and holler, "Lord! Give me a man!," say to yourself, "I can get a man, but in order to get the man of God chosen for me, I must first get in preparation for his coming." When the man of God finds you, which of the ten virgins will he encounter? Will you be one of the five whose lanterns were filled with oil and therefore were prepared to welcome the bridegroom? Or will you be one of the five who did not prepare and had to go out to buy more oil for their lanterns, which caused them to miss the bridegroom's arrival. Their lack of preparation resulted in their missing the wedding banquet.

This is your life and your future. Prepare to enjoy it.

In closing, I encourage you to learn to go to God first in all things. If you practice it now, it will become a habit later. Making friends, family, parents, and even your pastor, the first person you seek instead of

God, causes them to become a god in your life. If this happens, your relationship with God will change. Get to the place where God is your first teacher. God can teach you anything you need to know if you develop a relationship with Him. Allow Him to be your teacher. Consider Moses: God spoke directly to him. God was his teacher. Imagine how your life would change if you had half the relationship with God that Moses did. Getting a man is easy; but if you want a man after God's own heart, then you need to prepare. While you are preparing, I encourage you to meditate on this word from Psalms 27:14: Wait on the LORD; BE STRONG AND TAKE HEART AND WAIT ON THE LORD. And may the blessings of God follow you to overtake you until we meet again; either on this side of the pen or face to face.

You Can't Afford Me by Monica L. Baker

You can't afford me!

I was bought at a price.

Minimum charge: Lay down your life,

Shed your blood, get beaten beyond recognition;

Pay all my debts to a zero balance; hang on a tree;

Then forgive your assailants. You can't do that for me,

Let's face it. You haven't even mastered getting through,

Through a sentence without telling a lie.

You don't love me enough to be willing to die.

So I cannot forfeit the price that was paid when

The one who loves me got up from his grave

For me, his suffering was not in vain.

I lift up my hands and call out his name;

And he answers me every single time that I call;

Picks me up every single time that I fall.

So I have to refuse what you're offering me;

It's not befitting for a child of the King!

No! I will not let you call me out of my name,

Make a fool of me; try to reduce me to shame.

I know who I am and to whom I belong;

I don't have to settle and be treated wrong.

You cannot afford me,

I was bought at a price that is out of your range;

It would cost you your life!

them that they were self-conscious about and they were looking for a man to make them feel better about themselves.

I have also had relationships with women in Spain, Italy, Germany, Asia, and up and down the entire eastern coast. I dated large and small women from almost every ethnic background. I believe the only culture of women I did not date was the Eskimo and Aborigine. I also did not date women whose fathers had an active role in their lives, or virgins. Interesting, don't you think? What is even more interesting is that I married Mamie Fay. God has a sense of humor.

By the time I had finally accepted Christ into my life, I had been romantically involved with many, many women. I can see you. Close your mouth. I am trying to be transparent here. I am ashamed of the man I used to be. It is something how you can feel so right by doing something so wrong. The devil had me feeling so good about being a whore mongering, womanizing fool. I was influenced by demonic spirits. I caused so much hurt and pain. I thank God for his mercy. When I received God's forgiveness, I was like the woman who wiped Jesus' feet with her hair.

"Then Mary took about a pint of pure nard, and expensive perfume; she poured it on Jesus' feet and wiped his feet with her hair. And the house was filled with the fragrance of the perfume."(John 12:3)

I believe my wife's "Get Yourself Together" class works very well with the singles who have taken it. The ladies first learn how to identify their weaknesses and then they work on them. When a woman identifies and then rectifies her weaknesses, it disarms the predator of his weapons he had set to use against her. By recognizing her true worth, the woman no longer needs a man to validate her because she has learned to validate herself!

Ladies, don't waste your time in the giving of yourself, physically or emotionally, to a man who is just not ready for a wife. I was engaged three times. I wanted to be married but I wasn't ready for a wife. (Some of you will get a revelation of that later.) I was so used to preying on women, being something I wasn't but what she wanted me to be, that there was no way I was ready for marriage. I didn't even know what love was until after I had given my life to Christ. Since then, I have had a lot of time to reflect on my life and past experiences. I have spent many hours praying and repenting.

I am now a happily married man with four daughters and a son. Like I said, God has a sense of humor.

At one point in my life, I was a wolf and a predator that preyed on the weaknesses of women. I was once a wolf in sheep's clothing but now I am a shepherd to the sheep.

"We were therefore buried with him through baptism into death in order that, just as Christ was raised from the dead through the glory of the Father, we too may live a new life. For if we have been united with him in a death like his, we will certainly also be united with him in a resurrection like his. For we know that our old self was crucified with him so that the body ruled by sin might be done away with, that we should no longer be slaves to sin—because anyone who has died has been set free from sin."(Romans 6:4-7)

Ladies, before closing, I would like to leave this nugget with you. A lot of men are just not ready for marriage. Why? Because they are afraid of commitment, especially African-American men. The older they get the more difficult it is for them to commit. When they do commit, they have very high standards.

There is an old saying that goes, "Why buy the cow when you can get the milk for free?" I am sad to say that this proverb is visible in the church today. Men and women are masquerading as husband and wife so they won't be judged by their peers when in truth they are enjoying the benefits of marriage without the certificate or the godly covenant. I have had friends who have confessed that they are not getting married "anytime soon" and yet they have woman, a companion, by their side that is willing to compromise who she is. I cannot say why women compromise and settle, but don't let this be you. Becoming someone's girlfriend is not biblical. In fact, when Jesus spoke with the woman at the well who had "five" husbands, he commanded her to "Go, call your husband and come back. "I have no husband," she replied. Jesus said to her, "You are right when you say you have no husband. The fact is, you have had five husbands, and the man you now have is not your husband." (John 4; 16-18)

Woman of God, come out from among them and "sin no more." (John 8:11)